Brad Miser

Sams **Teach Yourself**

iCloud®

in **10 Minutes**

Second Edition

800 East 96th Street, Indianapolis, Indiana 46240

ISBN-10: 0-67-23369-52
ISBN-13: 978-0-67-23369-59

Library of Congress Control Number: 2013935869

Printed in the United States of America

First Printing June 2013

Trademarks

All terms mentioned in this book that are known to be trademarks or service marks have been appropriately capitalized. Sams Publishing cannot attest to the accuracy of this information. Use of a term in this book should not be regarded as affecting the validity of any trademark or service mark.

Warning and Disclaimer

Every effort has been made to make this book as complete and as accurate as possible, but no warranty or fitness is implied. The information provided is on an "as is" basis. The author(s) and the publisher shall have neither liability nor responsibility to any person or entity with respect to any loss or damages arising from the information contained in this book or from the use of the CD or programs accompanying it.

Bulk Sales

Sams Publishing offers excellent discounts on this book when ordered in quantity for bulk purchases or special sales. For more information, please contact

U.S. Corporate and Government Sales
1-800-382-3419
corpsales@pearsontechgroup.com

For sales outside of the U.S., please contact

International Sales
international@pearsoned.com

Editor-in-Chief
Greg Wiegand

Sr. Acquisitions Editor
Laura Norman

Development Editor
Lora Baughey

Technical Editor
Greg Kettell

Managing Editor
Kristy Hart

Project Editor
Elaine Wiley

Copy Editor
Bart Reed

Indexer
Erika Millen

Proofreader
Sarah Kearns, Water Crest Publishing

Editorial Assistant
Cindy Teeters

Interior Designer
Gary Adair

Cover Designer
Mike Shirar

Compositor
Nonie Ratcliff

Table of Contents

About the Author

Brad Miser has written extensively about technology, with his favorite topics being Apple's amazing "i" technology, including iPods, iPhones, and iCloud. In addition to *Sams Teach Yourself iCloud, 2nd Edition*, books Brad has written include: *My iPod touch, 4th Edition*; *My iPhone, 6th Edition*; and *iTunes and iCloud for iPhones, iPads, and Pod touches Absolute Beginner's Guide*. He has also been an author, development editor, or technical editor on more than 50 other titles.

Brad is or has been a sales support specialist, the director of product and customer services, and the manager of education and support services for several software development companies. Previously, he was the lead proposal specialist for an aircraft engine manufacturer, a development editor for a computer book publisher, and a civilian aviation test officer/engineer for the U.S. Army. Brad holds a Bachelor of Science degree in mechanical engineering from California Polytechnic State University at San Luis Obispo and has received advanced education in maintainability engineering, business, and other topics.

Originally from California, Brad now lives in Brownsburg, Indiana, with his wife Amy; their three daughters, Jill, Emily, and Grace; a rabbit; and a sometimes-inside cat.

Brad would love to hear about your experiences with this book (the good, the bad, and the ugly). You can write to him at bradmiser@icloud.com.

Dedication

To those who have given the last full measure of devotion so the rest of us can be free.

Acknowledgments

A special thanks to Laura Norman, Acquisitions Editor extraordinaire, for involving me in this project. I appreciate the efforts of Lora Baughey, Development Editor, for ensuring the content of this book is meaningful and does allow you to learn iCloud in 10 minutes. Thanks to Greg Kettell, the Technical Editor, who made sure this book is accurate and "tells it like it is." Bart Reed deserves special mention for transforming my gibberish into readable text. And Elaine Wiley deserves kudos for the difficult task of coordinating all the many pieces, people, and processes required to make a book happen. Last, but certainly not least, to the rest of the important folks on the team, including Cindy Teeters, Gary Adair, and the rest of the top-notch Sams staff, I offer a sincere thank you for all of your excellent work on this project.

We Want to Hear from You!

As the reader of this book, *you* are our most important critic and commentator. We value your opinion and want to know what we're doing right, what we could do better, what areas you'd like to see us publish in, and any other words of wisdom you're willing to pass our way.

We welcome your comments. You can email or write to let us know what you did or didn't like about this book—as well as what we can do to make our books better.

Please note that we cannot help you with technical problems related to the topic of this book.

When you write, please be sure to include this book's title and author as well as your name and email address. We will carefully review your comments and share them with the author and editors who worked on the book.

Email: consumer@samspublishing.com

Mail: Sams Publishing
            ATTN: Reader Feedback
            800 East 96th Street
            Indianapolis, IN 46240 USA

Reader Services

Visit our website and register this book at informit.com/register for convenient access to any updates, downloads, or errata that might be available for this book.

Introduction

We all live in a connected world, and most of us use multiple devices, such as iPhones, iPads, Macintosh computers, and Windows PCs. Using multiple devices for similar functions, such as email or working on documents, presents the challenge of keeping all our devices in sync so that we have the same information, such as calendars and emails, available to us no matter which particular device we happen to be using at any point in time.

Enter iCloud.

Apple's iCloud service provides an Internet "cloud" on which you can store all sorts of information and documents. Each of your devices can then connect to the cloud so they all have access to the same information, photos, music, documents, and other types of data. The flow of information goes both ways, too: Changes you make on a device move to the cloud to update its information (which in turn is communicated to the other devices connected to your area in the cloud).

iCloud enables you to manage and sync all sorts of information and documents. It helps with your music, books, apps, and TV shows, too, because the content you purchase from the iTunes Store is automatically downloaded to all your devices and is retrievable whether you are using an iOS device or a computer. iCloud's Photo Stream stores your photos on the cloud where your devices can automatically access or store them. And, with the optional iTunes Match service, all the music in your iTunes Library is available to any of your iOS devices from the cloud—no syncing required.

iCloud is a great extension of your digital self onto the Internet. It makes all your devices much more effective, and even more fun, to use.

About This Book

Similar to the other books in the *Sams Teach Yourself in 10 Minutes* series, the purpose of this book is to enable you to learn how to use iCloud quickly and easily—and, hopefully, you'll even enjoy yourself along the way! This book is composed of a series of lessons, and each lesson covers a specific topic related to the use of iCloud. For example, Lesson 2, "Configuring iCloud on an iPhone, iPod touch, or iPad," teaches you how to set up iCloud on iOS devices, whereas Lesson 11, "Using iCloud with Your Calendars," shows you how to take advantage of iCloud to help you manage your calendars.

The lessons generally build on each other, starting with the more fundamental topics covered in the earlier lessons and moving toward more advanced topics in the later lessons. In general, if you work from the front of the book toward the back, your iCloud education progresses smoothly. You need to start with Lesson 1, "Getting Started with Your iCloud Account and Website," to establish your iCloud base. From there, move on to the lessons that explain how to set up iCloud on the devices you use. Lesson 3, "Configuring iCloud on Macintosh Computers," explains how to set up iCloud on a Mac, and Lesson 4, "Configuring iCloud on Windows Computers," explains how to do the same on a Windows PC. After you have those bases covered, you can jump to the other lessons based on your areas of interest.

The lessons include both information and explanations along with step-by-step tasks. You get more out of the lessons if you perform the steps as you read the lessons. Figures are included to show you what key steps look like on your devices' screens.

Who This Book Is For

This book is for anyone who wants to get the most out of iCloud. Although iCloud is well designed and relatively easy to use, you'll learn faster with this guide to help you. If you've never used iCloud, this book gets you started and helps you move toward becoming an iCloud guru. If you've previously dabbled with iCloud, this book helps you go beyond basic tasks and prepares you to use all of iCloud's amazing functionality. If you've spent a fair amount of time using iCloud, this book provides lessons to round out your iCloud expertise.

What Do I Need to Use This Book?

To make use of the information in this book, you need an iCloud account. Lesson 1 teaches you to create your own free account. You also need at least one device that can access iCloud; this can be an iOS device (iPhone, iPad, or iPod touch), a Mac, or a Windows PC. Your experience improves if you have more than one device, such as an iPad and a computer. If you are lucky enough to have more than two devices, even better!

In addition to the technical requirements, you just need a sense of adventure and curiosity to explore all this book offers you. iCloud is fun to use and, with this guide to help you, it should be fun to learn as well.

Conventions Used in This Book

Whenever you need to click a particular button or link or make a menu selection, you see the name of that item in **bold**, such as in "Click the **Save** button to save your document." You also find three special elements (Notes, Tips, and Cautions) throughout this book.

NOTE

A note provides information that adds to the knowledge you gain through each lesson's text and figures.

TIP

Tips offer alternate ways to do something, such as keyboard shortcuts, or they point out additional features of which you can take advantage.

CAUTION

You won't find many of these in this book, but when you do come across one, you should carefully read it to avoid problems or situations that could cause you grief, time, or money.

Sidebar

Sidebars provide additional information similar to a note, but sidebars are a bit longer and more detailed. Also like notes, you can skip over sidebars, but you'll benefit from absorbing the information they contain as part of your iCloud education.

LESSON 1

Getting Started with Your iCloud Account and Website

In this lesson, you get an overview of iCloud, learn how to obtain an account, and explore how you can use your iCloud website.

Understanding iCloud

iCloud is a service that connects your iOS devices (iPhones, iPads, or iPod touches), Macintosh computers, Windows computers, and Apple TVs to a "cloud," which is a central repository for data storage that is available on the Internet. Each device stores data on the cloud and receives data from the cloud. This enables all your devices to share the same information.

NOTE: **iOS Device**

An iOS device runs Apple's iOS operating system software. An iOS device is an iPhone, iPod touch, or iPad. iCloud works very similarly on all these devices, which is why they are referred to together as iOS devices. When there are differences between them, you'll see those differences identified. (In the context of iCloud, there aren't many.)

The iCloud service manages the flow of data to and from each device through the syncing process, which happens automatically if your devices are configured to allow it.

The result is that you have the ability to access the same information from each device. For example, when you create a contact on an iPhone, that contact is stored on the iPhone and is also copied up to the cloud. From there, the new contact is automatically copied onto each device with which your iCloud account's contact information is synced, as shown in Figure 1.1. This ensures you have access to the same contact information on each of your devices.

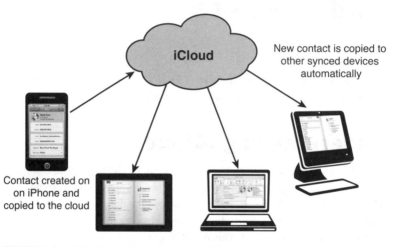

FIGURE 1.1 iCloud enables you to have the same data wherever you use it, including iOS devices, Macs, and Windows PCs.

In a similar way, iCloud can help you keep the following types of information in sync:

▶ Music, apps, and books that you purchase in the iTunes Store

▶ All the music in your iTunes Library (via the optional iTunes Match service)

▶ Photos (via Photo Stream)

▶ Documents

▶ Email

▶ Contacts

► Calendars

► Other information, such as web bookmarks and notes

NOTE: Documents

As explained in Lesson 8, "Using iCloud with Your Documents," iCloud only supports documents associated with specific applications. For example, when this lesson was written, iCloud document syncing worked natively within Pages, Numbers, and Keynote on iOS devices and Macs. The TextEdit, Preview, and GarageBand apps on Macs running OS X Mountain Lion also store documents directly on the cloud. You can use other applications, such as Word, with the downloaded versions of some documents (such as those from Pages and PDFs). Over time, other developers will add iCloud support for their applications so you will be able to use iCloud for your documents more broadly.

You can also use iCloud to help locate and protect your iOS devices and Mac computers through the Find My iPhone/iPod/iPad/Mac application. In addition to locating a device, you can lock devices or even remotely wipe their memories if you've lost control of them.

Another useful function of iCloud is the ability to back up your iOS devices so that you can restore them in case something bad happens.

And if that isn't enough for you, you also get access to your own iCloud website that has web applications you can use with your synced data, along with tools you can use to manage your iCloud account.

To use iCloud, you first need to accomplish the following two tasks:

1. Obtain an iCloud account. This is explained in the next section.

2. Configure your devices to use your iCloud account. To do this, you log in to your iCloud account and determine which type of information is synced on each device. This task is explained in Lesson 2, "Configuring iCloud on an iPhone, iPod touch, or iPad," Lesson 3, "Configuring iCloud on Macintosh Computers," and Lesson 4, "Configuring iCloud on Windows Computers."

After iCloud is set up on each device, you can start working with the various services it provides. Each of these is explained in a later lesson in this book. For example, you can learn how to use iCloud for email in Lesson 9, "Configuring Your iCloud Email."

You don't have to use all of the services iCloud offers, nor do you have to start using them all at the same time. You can pick and choose which services you want to use and when you want to use them. And not all devices support all services. For example, you can't use contacts or calendar syncing with an Apple TV because it doesn't offer tools to work with that kind of information.

The devices that work with iCloud are the following:

- ▶ **iOS 6 devices**—Any iPhone, iPod touch, or iPad running iOS 6 or later are fully iCloud compatible.

- ▶ **Macintosh computers**—To use iCloud on a Mac as described in this book, you must be running OS X, version 10.8.2 or later, along with iTunes 11 or later. If you want to use Photo Stream, you need to have iPhoto '11, version 9.4 or later, or Aperture, version 3.4 or later. You also need to have Safari 6 or later installed to use your iCloud website. To work with documents in the cloud, you need to have Pages 4.3, Numbers 2.3, or Keynote 5.3 or later installed on your Mac.

NOTE: **Versions, Versions**

If you are running versions of software older than those described in this list, some of iCloud's functionality may work just fine for you, but other features may not work. The information in the remainder of this book assumes you are running the versions listed here or newer. Also, the Windows information in this book is based on Windows 7. If you are running Windows 8, the steps and figures you see in this book may look slightly different on your computer, but will lead you to the same places. Also, iCloud works with other web browsers, such as Chrome, but for this book, the text and figures are based on Safari on a Mac or Internet Explorer on a Windows PC.

▶ **Windows computers**—iCloud works with Microsoft Windows 7 or 8; this book is based on Windows 7. You also need to install version 2.1.1 of the iCloud control panel or newer and have iTunes 11 or later installed. To have your calendars and contacts synced via iCloud, you need to have Outlook 2007 or 2010 installed. To sync your bookmarks, you need to have either Safari version 5.1.7 or later or Internet Explorer 9 or later. (Instructions for installing the iCloud control panel are provided in Lesson 4.)

▶ **Apple TV**—iCloud can be used with an Apple TV running software version 5.1 or later.

Obtaining an iCloud Account

To use iCloud, you need an iCloud account. The good news is that you may already have one. The even better news is that an iCloud account is free to obtain and use. A free account includes access to almost all the services described in the previous section, along with 5GB of online storage space.

NOTE: **iCloud Is Mostly Free**

To use iTunes Match, an annual fee is required. Also, if you want to increase your online disk space, you need to pay an annual fee. (Managing your online disk space is explained later in this book.)

If you have any of the following accounts, you already have an iCloud account and are ready to start using iCloud:

▶ **iTunes Store**—If you've ever shopped at the iTunes Store, you created an account with an Apple ID and password. You can use these to access iCloud and can skip ahead to the section "Using Your iCloud Website."

▶ **Apple Online Store**—As with the iTunes Store, if you made purchases from Apple's online store, you created an account with an Apple ID and password. You can use these to access iCloud and can skip ahead to the section "Using Your iCloud Website."

▶ **MobileMe/.Mac**—If you used these previous iterations of Apple's online services, you can use the same login information to access your iCloud account.

▶ **Find My iPhone**—If you obtained a free Find My iPhone account, you can log in to iCloud using the same Apple ID and can jump ahead to the section "Using Your iCloud Website."

NOTE: **Apple ID and iOS Devices**

The first time you started up a new iOS device or one that has been restored as a new device, you were prompted to create an Apple ID or sign in to an existing one. If you created an Apple ID or enabled iCloud at that time, you can skip to the section "Using Your iCloud Website." If you didn't create an account at that time, continue to the next section.

If you don't have one of these accounts already, obtaining an iCloud account is pretty simple. You can get one on an iOS device, a Mac, or via iTunes on any kind of computer.

Creating an iCloud Account on an iOS Device

To create an iCloud account on an iOS device, perform the following steps:

1. Tap **Settings** on the Home screen. The Settings app opens.

2. Tap **iCloud**.

3. Tap **Get a Free Apple ID**. You're prompted to enter your birthday, which is used to determine which services are available to you.

4. Use the select wheel to enter your birthday and then tap **Next**.

5. Enter your first name, last name, and then tap **Next**.

6. To use an email address that you already have as an Apple ID, tap **Use your current email address**. To create a new @icloud.com email address, tap **Get a free iCloud email address**.

7. Tap **Next**.

8. If you chose to create a new email address in step 6, skip to step 10.

9. Enter the email address you want to use, tap **Next**, and skip to step 12.

10. Enter the email address you would like to have and use as your Apple ID (you enter the part before the @) and then tap **Next**.

11. Confirm that the email address you created is the one you want to use by tapping **Create**. After you've created an Apple ID, you can't change it, so be careful about what you use. If the email address is currently being used as an Apple ID, you see a warning and you must change the email address you entered until you create one that is not already being used.

12. Enter the password you want to use with your Apple ID in the Password and Verify fields and then tap **Next**. (Note that this is not the same password as the one associated with an existing email address; the Apple ID password is specifically for your iCloud account.) If the password you created doesn't meet the requirements, a message appears explaining the problem; change the password until it is accepted.

13. Tap **Question** and then tap the first security question you want to use to be able to gain access to your account should you forget your Apple ID information.

14. Enter the answer to your first security question.

15. Repeat steps 13 and 14 to create two more security questions.

16. Tap **Next**.

17. If you have another email address that you want to be able to use to regain access to your account should you forget your credentials, enter it on the Rescue Email screen and tap **Next**. This is optional, but is recommended.

18. If you don't want to receive emails from Apple, set the **Email Updates** switch to OFF and tap **Next**.

19. Review the terms and conditions and tap **Agree**. (If you don't agree with these, you won't be able to use iCloud.)

20. Tap **Agree** again. Your account is created and you're prompted to allow iCloud to use the device's location information, as shown in Figure 1.2.

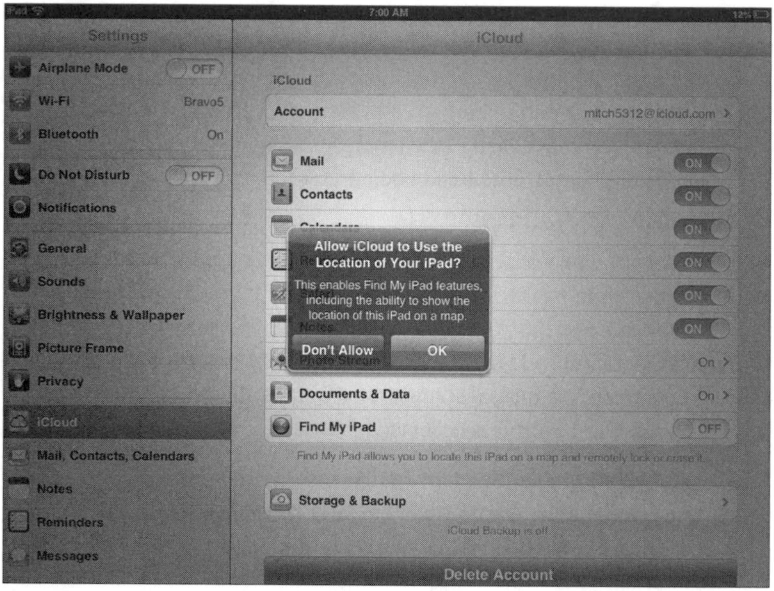

FIGURE 1.2   After you create a new Apple ID, you're prompted to allow iCloud to track your device's location.

21. Tap **OK** to allow your device's location to be tracked. If you don't allow this, you won't be able to use the Find My Device service to locate the device. Therefore, in most cases, you should allow it.

Your account is created and you can log in to it on the device. It is now ready to be used.

If you used an existing email, a confirmation email is sent to that address. When you click the link in that confirmation email, your Apple ID and iCloud account become active.

If you provided a rescue email account, you receive an email message that enables you to verify that this is the correct address to use.

After your iCloud account has been created and the email addresses verified, you can skip to the section "Using Your iCloud Website."

TIP: **Yet Another Way**

You can also use the My Apple ID website (located at appleid.apple. com) to create an Apple ID. As you learn later in this lesson, you can use this website to reset your password or find out what your Apple ID is as well.

Obtaining an iCloud Account on a Mac

You can create an iCloud account through the iCloud control pane of the System Preferences application as follows:

1. Open the System Preferences application.

2. Click the **iCloud** icon. The iCloud pane opens.

3. Click **Create an Apple ID**.

4. Follow the onscreen instructions to complete the process.

When finished, you are logged in to your new iCloud account and can skip to the section "Using Your iCloud Website."

Creating an iCloud Account via the iTunes Store

You can use an Apple ID to make purchases in the iTunes Store. You can use iTunes on a Mac or Windows PC to create an Apple ID for the store, which also creates your iCloud account. Here's how:

> NOTE: **Caveats**
>
> If you want to create a new email address to use with iCloud, don't use the iTunes method. Instead, create the account using an iOS device or by using the appleid.apple.com website. Although using iCloud is free, you have to provide payment information to create an iTunes Store account. If you don't want to provide this, use one of the other methods to create your account.

1. Open iTunes.

2. Click the **iTunes Store** button located in the upper-right corner of the iTunes window. iTunes connects to the Internet and moves into the iTunes Store. The iTunes Store appears in the iTunes window.

3. Click the **Sign In** button located in the upper-left corner of the iTunes Store window. The Sign In dialog appears (see Figure 1.3).

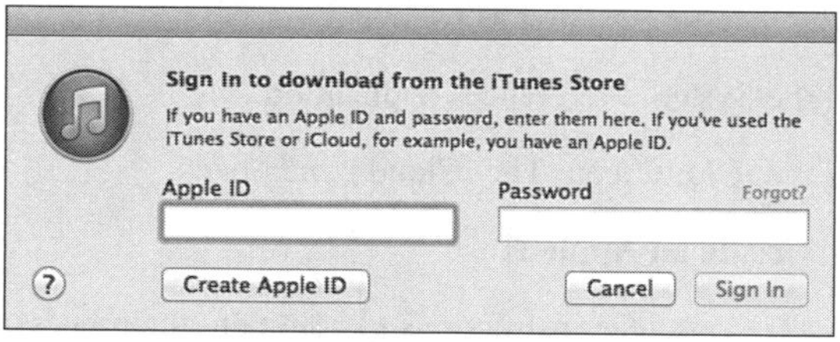

Sign In to download from the iTunes Store

If you have an Apple ID and password, enter them here. If you've used the iTunes Store or iCloud, for example, you have an Apple ID.

Apple ID   Password   Forgot?

[Create Apple ID]   [Cancel] [Sign In]

FIGURE 1.3 Use the Sign In dialog to start creating your Apple ID.

> NOTE: **Already In?**
> If you see an Apple ID instead of the Sign In link, iTunes is already logged in to an account. If the account is yours, skip to the section "Using Your iCloud Website." If the account shown isn't yours, click the account shown in the button and then click Sign Out so that you can create your account by performing step 3.

4. Click **Create Apple ID**. You move to the Welcome to the iTunes Store screen.

5. Click **Continue**.

6. Read the license agreement, check the **I have read and agree to these terms and conditions** check box, and click **Agree**.

7. Read the information and follow the onscreen instructions to provide the rest of the information required. This includes entering your primary and rescue email addresses (optional), creating a password, choosing security questions and answers, and providing credit card information.

8. After you've provided the required information, click **Create Apple ID**. An email is sent to the email address you provided for your account.

9. Switch to your email application and open the email you received on your primary address.

10. Click the **Verify Now** link in the verification email message you receive (see Figure 1.4). You move to the My Apple ID website.

11. Enter your email address in the Apple ID field.

12. Enter your password in the Password field.

13. Click **Verify Address**. If you are able to sign in, your Apple ID is ready to go, and you can use iCloud.

14. If you elected to provide a rescue email address, repeat steps 9 through 13, except this time open the verification email that is sent to your rescue address.

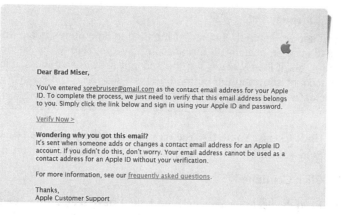

FIGURE 1.4   Apple sends this email to the address associated with your Apple ID to confirm that you did create an account.

> NOTE: **Rescue Me!**
>
> A rescue address is used to communicate with you if you lose access to your primary email address.

Using Your iCloud Website

With your iCloud account, you get a useful website too. The website has applications you can use for your email, contacts, and calendars. You can also use the Find My Device feature to locate a device and to secure it if it is out of your control. Also, you can store and access documents there. All of these features are covered in later lessons.

In this section, you learn how to access your website, choose applications, and manage your iCloud account.

To get the best experience with your iCloud website on a Mac, you should use one of the following web browsers:

- ▶ Safari, version 6 or later
- ▶ Firefox, version 16 or later
- ▶ Chrome, version 23 or later

To make the most of your iCloud website on a Windows PC, you should use one of the following web browsers:

► Safari, version 5.1.7 or later

► Internet Explorer, version 9 or later

► Firefox, version 16 or later

► Chrome, version 23 or later

NOTE: **Your Mileage May Vary**

The remaining text and figures in this lesson and throughout other lessons are based on Safari on a Mac or Internet Explorer on a Windows PC. If you use a different web browser, the screens and steps may be slightly different for you.

Logging In to Your iCloud Website

Logging in to your iCloud website isn't challenging, as you can see:

1. Use a web browser to move to icloud.com.

2. Enter your **Apple ID**, which is the email associated with your iCloud account.

3. Enter your **Apple ID password**.

4. To save your information on the computer so you can move directly into your website when you come back to this address, check the **Keep me signed in** check box, as shown in Figure 1.5.

5. Click the **right-facing arrow** or press **Enter** or **Return**. You log in to your website and work with your web applications or manage your account.

FIGURE 1.5   You can remain signed in to your iCloud website to make it even easier to access.

Working with iCloud Web Applications

When you first log in to your website, you see icons for each of the iCloud applications, as shown in Figure 1.6. The icons are labeled, so it's easy to tell what they do even if you don't recognize them.

FIGURE 1.6   Click an application's icon to work with it.

In the upper-right corner of the window, you see your name, the Sign Out link, and the Help button (?).

To do some additional configuration of your account, click your name. The Account dialog box appears. Use the following steps to adjust your account settings:

1. Click the image located at the top of the dialog box and choose the image you want to associate with your account. If you are using a computer with a camera, you can take a photo of yourself or you can choose a file on your computer's desktop.

> **NOTE: Plug Me In**
> When you change your account's image, you may be prompted to install a plugin. Just follow the onscreen instructions to do so and you'll be able to change your account's image.

2. To change the language the site uses, click the language currently shown and then click the language you want to use.

3. To set the time zone, click the time zone currently shown, click the city shown in the button, and then click the city associated with the time zone you want to use. That time zone is set for your website.

4. Click **Notifications**. The Notification options appear, as shown in Figure 1.7.

5. Set the switch to ON for any notifications you want to receive or to OFF if you don't want to receive notifications. For example, if you don't want to receive a notification for reminders you create, set the **Reminders** switch so it shows OFF.

6. Click the **return** button located in the upper-left corner of the dialog box, which is labeled with your Apple ID.

7. Click **Done**.

If you want to sign out of your website, such as if someone else is going to be using the computer, click the **Sign Out** link.

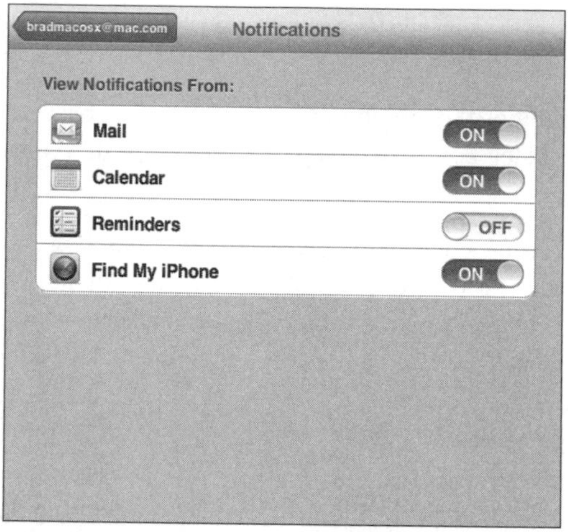

FIGURE 1.7   Use these settings to determine when you receive iCloud notifications.

You can get iCloud help by clicking the **Help** button.

To use an application, simply click its icon, and you move into that application; Figure 1.8 shows the Contacts application as an example.

To change applications, click the **Cloud** button located in the upper-left corner of the current application's window. You move back to the screen shown in Figure 1.6 and can choose a different application by clicking its icon.

NOTE: **Going Back Where You've Been**

Whenever you move back to your icloud.com website, you move back into the application you used most recently. Click the Cloud button to see the icons for the other applications and switch to any of them.

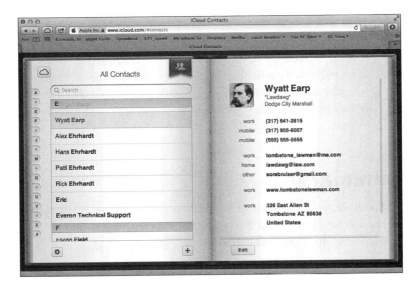

FIGURE 1.8   Here, you see the iCloud Contacts application.

Managing Your Account and Apple ID

To manage your account, if you ever forget your Apple ID or password, or if you want to reset your password, you can use the My Apple ID website.

To access it, use a web browser to move to appleid.apple.com. Here, you can do the following:

▶ To create a new Apple ID, click the **Create an Apple ID** button and follow the onscreen instructions.

▶ If you think you have an Apple ID but aren't sure, click the **Find your Apple ID** link and follow the onscreen instructions.

▶ To reset your password, click the **Reset your password** link and follow the onscreen instructions.

▶ To manage your account, click **Manage your account**. Sign in to your account. Here, you can change various aspects of your account, including your identification and email addresses, password and security information, addresses, phone numbers, and language and contact preferences. To edit an area, you click its link along the left side of the window; the tools you use to make changes appear in the right side of the window.

Summary

In this lesson, you learned about iCloud, how to obtain an iCloud account, and how to sign in to your iCloud website. In the next lesson, you learn how to configure iCloud on an iOS device.

LESSON 2

Configuring iCloud on an iPhone, iPod touch, or iPad

In this lesson, you learn how to set up an iPhone, iPod touch, or iPad to use iCloud.

Configuring iCloud on an iOS Device

iCloud was designed for Apple's iOS devices: iPhone, iPod touch, and iPad. As you learned in Lesson 1, "Getting Started with Your iCloud Account and Website," when you configure an iCloud account on one of these devices, you get all kinds of benefits, such as syncing your information across multiple devices, online backup, and so on.

The iCloud software is built in to the iOS software, so all you need to do is to configure your iOS device to access your iCloud account. The steps to do this are nearly identical on an iPhone, iPod touch, and iPad. Of course, the screens look slightly different on each device, but the steps to configure iCloud are exactly the same, so you can follow along no matter which device you are using.

In some cases, you see the name of a specific kind of device in a figure or command, such as Find My iPhone. Rather than repeat each option (Find My iPhone, Find My iPod, or Find My iPad), the text includes just one of the terms. If you are using a different device, you see that device's name instead. For example, if you are using an iPad, you see Find My iPad, whereas if you are using an iPhone, you see Find My iPhone instead.

Configuring an iOS device to use iCloud is a two-part process. The first part is to do the basic configuration of your iCloud account. The second part is to determine how and when information is synced between the cloud and your device. These topics are covered in the following two sections.

You can also perform advanced configuration of your iCloud account. This is optional and is covered in the next-to-last section of this lesson.

Performing Basic iCloud Configuration on an iOS Device

To configure your iCloud account on an iOS device, perform the following steps:

1. On the Home screen, tap **Settings**. The Settings app opens.

2. Tap **iCloud**. You move to the iCloud Settings screen. You're prompted to enter your iCloud account information, as shown in Figure 2.1.

3. Enter your Apple ID. If you previously used the same iCloud account on the device, this may be entered already.

4. Enter your Apple ID password.

5. Tap **Sign In**, and your iCloud account is configured on your device.

6. If you're prompted about merging information already in your iCloud account, tap **Don't Merge** if you don't want the information already on your device to be moved into your iCloud account. Tap **Merge** if you do.

> NOTE: **Merging Information**
>
> If you previously synced information under your iCloud account, such as calendars, when you enable syncing for that information, you may be prompted with the options Merge and Don't Merge. If you tap Merge, the information you previously synced combines with the information already stored in your iCloud account. If you choose

Don't Merge, you are prompted to Keep or Delete. If you tap Keep, the information you previously synced is kept on the device. If you tap Delete and then tap Delete again at the warning prompt, the information you previously synced is deleted from the device.

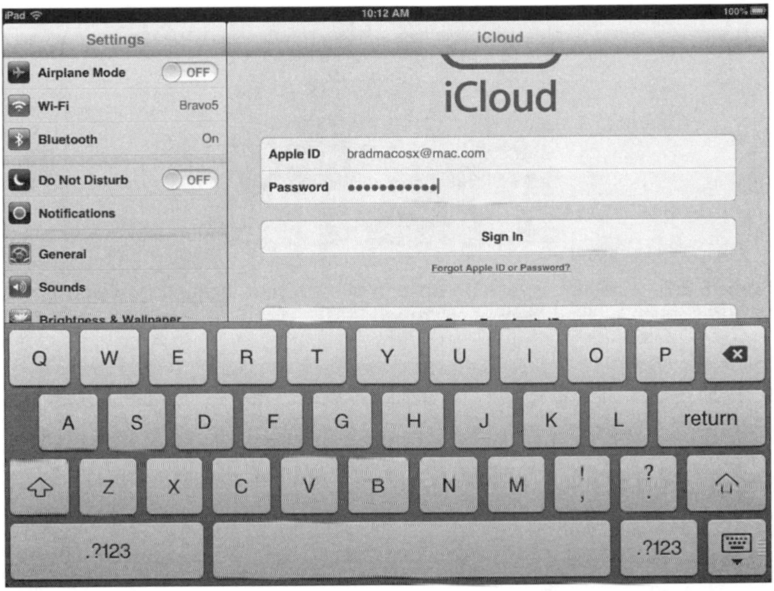

FIGURE 2.1   Enter your Apple ID and password and then tap Sign In to access your iCloud account.

7. If you're prompted as shown in Figure 2.2, tap **OK** to allow iCloud to access your device's location or **Don't Allow** if you don't want this to happen. You need to allow this for some features, such as Find My iPhone, to work. Next, you see the screen that enables you to choose the type of information you want to sync on your device.

8. Set the slider to the ON position next to each kind of information you want to sync on your device, as shown in Figure 2.3; for example, if **Mail** is set to ON, email syncs between your iCloud account and the device. If you set a slider to the OFF position,

that type of information won't sync between your iCloud account and the device. As an example of this, suppose you don't want your iCloud calendar information to appear on the device; set the **Calendars** switch to OFF, and that information is excluded.

FIGURE 2.2   iCloud needs to be able to access your location for some features, such as Find My iPhone, to work.

Settings	iCloud
Airplane Mode OFF	iCloud
Wi-Fi Bravo5	Account bradmacosx@mac.com >
Bluetooth On	Mail ON
Do Not Disturb OFF	Contacts ON
Notifications	Calendars ON
General	Reminders ON
Sounds	Safari ON
Brightness & Wallpaper	Notes ON
Picture Frame	Photo Stream On >
Privacy	Documents & Data On >
iCloud	Find My iPad ON
Mail, Contacts, Calendars	Find My iPad allows you to locate this iPad on a map and remotely lock or erase it.
Notes	Storage & Backup >
Reminders	iCloud Backup is off.
Messages	Delete Account

FIGURE 2.3   When a slider is set to ON, the corresponding type of information is included in the sync process.

Table 2.1 lists each of the options and provides a reference where you can find a detailed explanation of using each type of information in this book.

TABLE 2.1 iCloud Sync Options

Information	Description	Where to Find More Information
Mail	iCloud email	Lesson 9, "Configuring Your iCloud Email"
Contacts	Contact information	Lesson 10, "Using iCloud to Manage Your Contacts"
Calendars	Calendars	Lesson 11, "Using iCloud with Your Calendars"
Reminders	Reminders (tasks in Outlook)	Lesson 12, "Using iCloud to Sync Other Information"
Bookmarks	Safari or Internet Explorer bookmarks	Lesson 12, "Using iCloud to Sync Other Information"
Notes	Text notes	Lesson 12, "Using iCloud to Sync Other Information"
Photo Stream	Stores photos in the cloud	Lesson 7, "Using iCloud with Your Photos"
Documents & Data	Stores documents and other data in the cloud	Lesson 8, "Using iCloud with Your Documents"
Find My iPhone	Allows you to track your device's location	Lesson 13, "Using iCloud to Locate and Secure Your Devices"
Storage & Backup	Backs up the information on your device in the cloud and enables you to manage your online storage space	Lesson 14, "Using iCloud to Back Up and Restore Devices"

NOTE: **The Missing Sliders**
As you can see in Figure 2.3, Photo Stream and Documents & Data don't have sliders. When you tap those items, you move to screens that provide additional controls, which include controls to configure specific aspects of that service, such as to enable or disable photo sharing on your Photo Stream.

9. Tap **iCloud**. Your iCloud account configuration is complete. Next, determine how and when your iCloud information is updated on your device.

NOTE: **To Keep or Delete? That Is the Question**

If you move one of the sliders to the OFF position, you're prompted to keep the current data or delete it. For example, if you have previously used Calendar syncing, but then turn it OFF, you're prompted to keep or delete the calendar information. If you keep the data, it remains on your device, but is not updated on the cloud. If you delete the data, it is removed from the device, but the information on the cloud remains.

NOTE: **To Merge or Not? That Is Also the Question**

If you reenable information while syncing that was previously not synced, you may be prompted to merge or delete the information on your device. When you choose the Merge option, the data on the device combines with that in the cloud. If you choose Delete, the information on the device is replaced with that from the cloud.

Configuring Information Updates on an iOS Device

When you connect to the cloud via your iCloud account, information moves between the cloud and your devices. For example, you receive email messages in the cloud. When a device is configured to sync your email, new messages move from the server onto your device. Likewise, when you create email messages on your device, they move into the cloud.

There are three ways the information can move between your iOS devices and the cloud:

▶ **Push**—Push syncing occurs when the device is connected to the Internet and new information is created on either the device or in the cloud. The new information is moved to or from the cloud as soon as it exists; this keeps information on the iOS device the most current because what you see on the device always reflects what is in the cloud. Push syncing has one definite drawback and another that is a matter of opinion. The definite drawback is that Push causes the largest energy use and shortest working time before you need to recharge your device, especially if the data in the cloud changes frequently. The drawback that is a matter of opinion is that some people (myself included) find Push intrusive and disruptive because notifications of new information can be almost constant and distracting from the task you are currently working on. It can certainly be annoying to others if you have audible notifications and are in meetings or other group situations. That said, some people prefer to have new information on their devices as soon as possible and are willing to accept shorter times between charges and more frequent interruptions.

▶ **Fetch**—Fetch syncing is automatic but is done according to a schedule, such as every 30 minutes. This provides automatic syncing but uses significantly less battery power than Push. And because notifications only occur when the scheduled sync happens, it can be less intrusive and distracting than Push syncing.

▶ **Manual**—Manual syncing occurs only when you start the process by moving into the related app and when you refresh an app's information (typically by swiping down the screen). For example, when you open the Mail app, your device checks for new messages and downloads any that have been added to the cloud since the last time you checked. The downside of manual syncing is that you have to take action to sync your device. The upside is that you get information exactly when you want to deal with it. Unless you frequently sync manually, this option also uses the least battery power.

The option that is best for you depends on how much information you receive and whether or not you want to be immediately notified when you receive it. Because of improved battery life and automatic syncing, I recommend you start with the Fetch option. You can adjust the time intervals for syncing to ensure you get information to suit your preference while saving power compared to Push. You can always change or tweak the settings to suit your preferences over time.

To configure how syncing occurs, perform the following steps:

1. Tap **Settings** on the Home screen. The Settings app opens.

2. Tap **Mail, Contacts, Calendars**.

3. Tap **Fetch New Data**. You see the Fetch New Data screen, as shown in Figure 2.4.

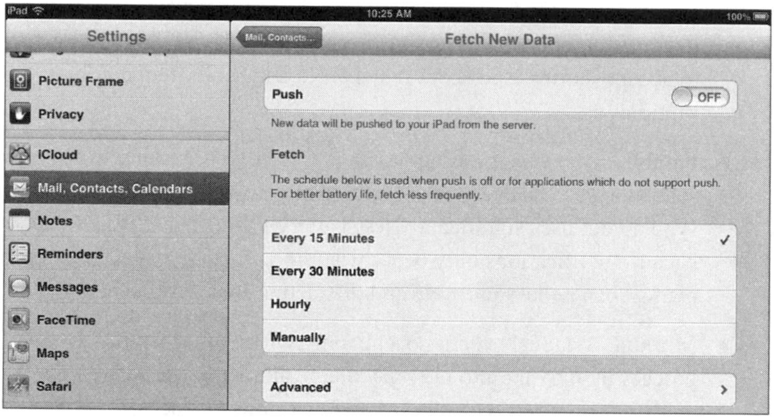

FIGURE 2.4   With these settings, this iPad mini syncs every 15 minutes.

4. If you want to use push syncing, set the **Push** slider to the ON position. This setting impacts all your wirelessly synced accounts. If you want to disable Push for all accounts, set the slider to the OFF position. Even if you enable Push, you need to configure the Fetch interval that is used when Push isn't available.

5. In the Fetch section, tap the amount of time when you want to sync information when Push is OFF or if it is not available for

specific accounts. The options are **Every 15 Minutes**, **Every 30 Minutes**, and **Hourly**.

6. If you want to use manual syncing only, tap **Manually**. If Push is ON, it overrules this setting, so if you choose only manual syncing, Push must be OFF, too. If Push is ON, the Manually option only applies when Push is not available. The iCloud account is ready to use, and its information syncs according to your settings.

TIP: Advanced Syncing

You can have multiple accounts configured on your devices. In addition to your iCloud account, you might also have Gmail, Exchange, and other types of accounts. The settings on the Fetch New Data screen apply to all your accounts. Tap Advanced on the Fetch New Data screen to see the Advanced screen. Here, you can configure the sync settings for each account individually by tapping the account. You move to that account's Select Schedule screen and then can tap Push, Fetch, or Manually. (If an account doesn't support push syncing, you won't see the Push option on its sync settings screen.) The setting on this screen applies only to that account. For example, you might want to have your work-related accounts sync automatically with Fetch and use manual syncing for your personal accounts.

Performing Advanced iCloud Account Configurations

The information in this section is optional, and you can probably do most of what you want with iCloud without ever using it. However, it's good to be aware of these options in case you'd like to tweak your account further.

To access these advanced options, do the following:

1. On the Home screen, tap **Settings**. The Settings app opens.

2. Tap **iCloud**. You move to the iCloud settings screen.

3. Tap **Account** at the top of the screen. The Account window pops up, as shown in Figure 2.5.

FIGURE 2.5   You can use this window to perform advanced configuration of your iCloud account.

This window consists of three sections:

▶ **iCloud Account Information**—Here, you can change or reenter your password and change the description of your account; the default name is iCloud, but you might want to change it to be your Apple ID or some other more personalized term.

▶ **Storage Plan**—This section provides your current iCloud storage; the default is 5GB. If you've upgraded your storage space, you see your current amount and what your annual fee is for this amount. If you tap the storage space icon, you can change the amount of space allowed under your account. If you tap **Payment Information**, you can change the payment details for your account.

▶ **Advanced**—This option enables you to further configure your iCloud email. The options available are explained in the following text.

If you tap **Mail** at the bottom of the screen, you can do even more configuration of your email account, as shown in Figure 2.6.

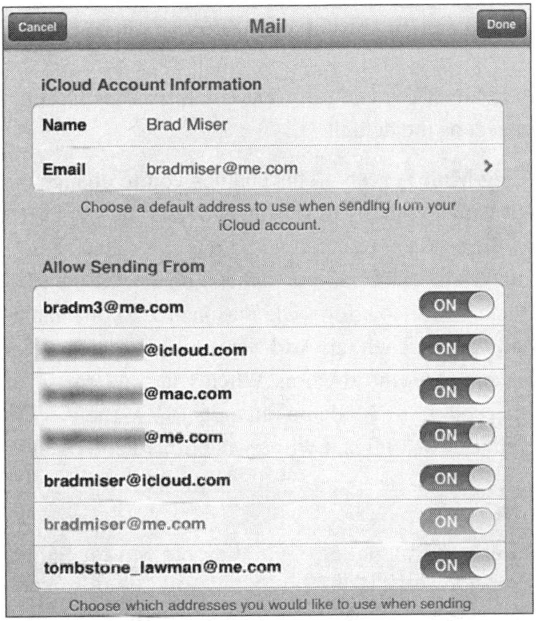

| Cancel | Mail | Done |

iCloud Account Information

| Name | Brad Miser |
| Email | bradmiser@me.com | > |

Choose a default address to use when sending from your iCloud account.

Allow Sending From

bradm3@me.com	ON
▉▉▉▉▉@icloud.com	ON
▉▉▉▉▉@mac.com	ON
▉▉▉▉▉@me.com	ON
bradmiser@icloud.com	ON
bradmiser@me.com	ON
tombstone_lawman@me.com	ON

Choose which addresses you would like to use when sending

FIGURE 2.6   The Mail window provides additional configuration for your iCloud email account.

The options you can configure on this window include the following (you may have to swipe up or down to see all of them):

▶ **Name**—This is the name shown in the From field in emails you send. The default is the name associated with your iCloud account, but you can change it to something else.

▶ **Email**—When you have more than one email account configured on the device, tap the **Email** line, tap the address that you
want to be the default when you create new messages, and tap
Mail to return to the Mail window. (You can easily choose a different account from which to send specific messages.)

▶ **Allow Sending From**—When you have multiple email
addresses, you can choose to allow or prevent email from being
sent from them. To prevent email from being sent, set the
address switch to OFF. To allow email to be sent, set the account
switch to ON. (You can't prevent email from being sent from the
account set as the default.)

▶ **Outgoing Mail Server**—This enables you to change the server
through which your email is sent. (You should not have to ever
change the server associated with your iCloud account.) You can
also add more SMTP servers that can be used if the iCloud
server is not available for some reason. To do this, tap **SMTP** on
the Mail screen. Then tap **Add Server** and enter the server's
address and other information. When you send email from your
iCloud account, the Mail app attempts to use the iCloud SMTP
server first. If that fails, it will try the other servers on the list.

> NOTE: **SMTP**
>
> In case you are wondering, SMTP is the acronym for Simple Mail
> Transfer Protocol, which is the protocol iCloud uses to send email
> messages. If you weren't wondering, never mind.

▶ **Archive Messages**—If you set the **Archive Messages** switch to
ON, messages you delete are saved in your iCloud's Archive
folder instead of the Trash folder. This option is useful if you
want to be able to delete email messages but always be able to
go back to them in the future. However, messages stored in the
Archive folder count against your iCloud storage space alloca-
tion. If you deal with a lot of messages and only have the default
5GB of storage space, your deleted messages can take up a significant amount of your space.

▶ **Advanced**—If you tap **Advanced** at the bottom of the Mail
  screen, you can set the behaviors of your mailboxes. These
  include where draft, sent, and deleted messages are stored, when
  deleted messages are removed from the server (the default is one
  week), and the S/MIME setting (see the following note).

You don't have to adjust any of these settings for your iCloud account to
work fine for you, but if you are interested in tweaking the configuration
further, be sure to check them out.

NOTE: **S/MIME**

Secure/Multipurpose Internet Mail Extensions (S/MIME) are a
means to encrypt emails so that a key is required to be able to
decrypt the information contained in them. To use S/MIME, you
must install a certificate on your device for any account that uses
these extensions. iCloud doesn't support this technology. If you do
have access to an account that supports S/MIME, you need the certificate, key, and configuration information from the account provider
to be able to configure it on your device.

Summary

In this lesson, you learned how to configure an iOS device to use iCloud
services. In the next lesson, you learn how to set up iCloud on a
Macintosh computer.

LESSON 3

Configuring iCloud on Macintosh Computers

In this lesson, you learn how to configure your iCloud account on a Macintosh computer.

Logging In to Your iCloud Account

The iCloud software is built in to OS X. To start using it, you simply need to log in to your iCloud account using the following steps:

> NOTE: **OS X, v 10.8.2 or Later**
>
> To use iCloud's full functionality, your Mac must be running OS X Mountain Lion, version 10.8.2 or later. If you are using an earlier version of Mountain Lion, you can upgrade by choosing Software Update on the Apple menu and then downloading and installing the update through the App Store application. If you aren't using OS X Mountain Lion yet, you can purchase it using the App Store application.

1. Open the System Preferences application.

2. Click **iCloud**. The iCloud pane opens, as shown in Figure 3.1.

3. Enter your Apple ID.

4. Enter your Apple ID password.

5. Click **Sign In**. Your Mac logs in to your iCloud account. You're prompted to use iCloud for specific syncing, as shown in Figure 3.2.

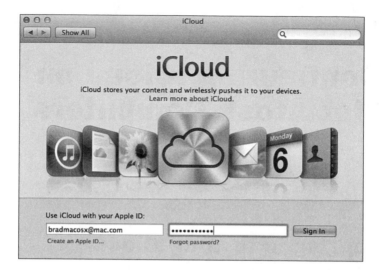

FIGURE 3.1 To start using iCloud on your Mac, log in to your iCloud account.

FIGURE 3.2 These settings enable or disable iCloud syncing for contacts, calendars, and other information as well as enable or disable Find My Mac.

6. If you don't want to sync information, uncheck the **Use iCloud for contacts, calendars, reminders, notes, and Safari** check box. You can configure this syncing more specifically later, so it doesn't matter all that much if you leave this enabled now or not.

7. Uncheck the **Use Find My Mac** check box if you don't want to use this service that can locate your Mac. If you disable it, you can choose to use this feature later by configuring it in the iCloud pane of the System Preferences application.

8. Click **Next**.

9. If you enabled Find My Mac, click **Allow** to allow iCloud to use Location Services to locate your Mac. iCloud services begin working, and the information you enabled is synced with your iCloud account. Now you're ready to perform more detailed configurations of your iCloud services.

NOTE: **No Prompt?**

If you aren't prompted to allow iCloud to use Location Services, those services may be disabled on your computer. Open the System Preferences app, double-click the **Security & Privacy** icon to open that pane, click the **Privacy** tab, select **Location Services**, and check the **Enable Location Services** check box. (You have to be authenticated as an administrator to do this.)

Configuring and Managing Your iCloud Services

You can configure and manage the iCloud services you use by completing the following steps:

1. Open the System Preferences application.

2. Click **iCloud**. The iCloud pane opens, as shown in Figure 3.3. In the right part of the pane, you see the iCloud services available on your Mac. If a service's check box is checked, that

information, such as Calendars & Reminders, is being synced with the cloud, or the service, such as Back to My Mac, is enabled on your computer. At the bottom of the pane, you see the iCloud Storage gauge that shows how much account space you are using, along with the Manage button (more on this shortly). In the left part of the pane, you see the Apple ID currently logged in and the buttons you can use to manage your iCloud account.

FIGURE 3.3   Use the iCloud pane to configure and manage iCloud services on your Mac.

3. To enable specific information to be included in the sync process or to activate a service, check its check box; if you uncheck a check box, that information is removed from the sync process or the service is disabled. Table 3.1 lists the options and shows you where to get additional related information.

TABLE 3.1   iCloud Options on a Mac

Information	Description	Where to Find More Information
Mail	iCloud email	Lesson 9, "Configuring Your iCloud Email" (email)
Contacts	Contact information	Lesson 10, "Using iCloud to Manage Your Contacts"
Calendars & Reminders	Calendars and reminders	Lesson 11, "Using iCloud with Your Calendars"
Notes	Notes in the Notes application on a Mac	Lesson 12, "Using iCloud to Sync Other Information"
Safari	Safari bookmarks	Lesson 12, "Using iCloud to Sync Other Information"
Photo Stream	Photo storage and sharing via iCloud	Lesson 7, "Using iCloud with Your Photos"
Documents & Data	Stores documents in the cloud so you can access them from multiple devices	Lesson 8, "Using iCloud with Your Documents"
Back to My Mac	Enables you to control your Mac over the Internet	"Using the Back to My Mac Feature," later in this lesson
Find My Mac	Allows you to track your Mac's current location and protect it in case you lose control of your computer	Lesson 13, "Using iCloud to Locate and Secure Your Devices"

Here are some other pointers to keep in mind as you work with the iCloud pane of the System Preferences application:

▶ When you disable information syncing by unchecking its check box, you're prompted to either keep or delete the iCloud information that is currently stored on your Mac. If you select the **Keep** option, the sync process is stopped, but the information that has previously been synced is removed from your computer. If you select the **Delete** option, the information from iCloud is removed from your computer.

▶ The gauge at the bottom of the pane (and the status information directly above it) shows how much iCloud storage space you are currently using. The more the bar is filled in, the less iCloud storage space you have available for new information. If you click the **Manage** button, the Manage Storage sheet appears, as shown in Figure 3.4. In the left pane of the window, you see the services and applications that are currently using storage space and how much space each is using. When you select an application, you see the items currently being stored for that application and how much space each is consuming. Click **Done** to close the sheet.

FIGURE 3.4   Here, you see how your iCloud disk space is being used.

TIP: **Freeing Space**
You can delete an item, such as a document, by selecting it and clicking **Delete**. You can delete all the items for an application by selecting the application and clicking **Delete All**. Of course, you don't want to do either of these unless you are sure you don't need the items any more or you have them stored in a different location.

▶ If you click the **Manage** button and then click the **View Account** button on the Manage Storage sheet (you may be prompted to provide your Apple ID password), you see various aspects of your account, such as your current storage plan, payment information, and country/region. You can change these by clicking the **Change** or **Edit** button and using the resulting screens to make and save your changes. Click **Done** to close the Manage Storage sheet.

▶ If you click the **Account Details** button on the iCloud pane, a sheet showing your name and a description of your iCloud account appears. You can change this information by editing it and clicking **OK**. This doesn't impact your account itself, but does change how information about the account appears, such as the name shown in the From field on emails you send.

▶ You can sign out of your iCloud account by clicking **Sign Out**. You're prompted to keep or delete the iCloud information currently on your Mac. When you have indicated what you want to do with each type of information, you are logged out of your iCloud account. The iCloud pane returns to the one that allows you to sign in to your account. You can sign back in to your account or sign in to a different iCloud account.

NOTE: **One iCloud Account at a Time**

Although it's possible for you to have more than one iCloud account, you can only use one at a time for each user account on your Mac. To change the iCloud account you are currently using, sign out of one and then sign in to a different one.

Using the Back to My Mac Feature

The Back to My Mac feature enables you to access your Mac over the Internet. To use Back to My Mac, the following conditions must be true:

▶ You must be logged in to the same iCloud account on your current Mac and the computer you are going to access via Back to My Mac.

▶ Back to My Mac must be enabled on the computer you are going to access and the computer you are currently using.

▶ To access files stored on the Mac from a different computer, File Sharing must be enabled on the Sharing pane of the System Preferences application.

▶ To be able to control the Mac from a different computer, Screen Sharing on the Sharing page of the System Preferences application must be enabled.

▶ The computer you are accessing must be running, your user account must be logged in, and the computer can't be sleeping. (Ensure the **Wake for network access** check box on the Energy Saver pane is selected.)

When these conditions are met, you can access the computer by selecting it in the SHARED section of the sidebar in a Finder window. You can click **Connect As** to log in to that computer to access its files and folders or click **Share Screen** to control the computer from your current computer.

Summary

In this lesson, you learned how to set up your iCloud account on a Macintosh computer. In the next lesson, you learn how to configure your iCloud account on a Windows PC.

LESSON 4

Configuring iCloud on Windows Computers

In this lesson, you learn how to configure your iCloud account on a Windows computer.

Downloading and Installing the iCloud Control Panel

To use iCloud with a Windows PC, you need to download and install the latest version of the iCloud control panel. Here's how to do this with Internet Explorer (the steps for other web browsers will be similar):

1. Open a web browser and go to http://support.apple.com/kb/DL1455.

2. Click **Download**.

3. At the prompt, click **Run**. The software is downloaded to your computer and then the installer runs.

4. Click **Run** at the prompt.

5. Follow the onscreen instructions to complete the installation of the iCloud control panel. You have to accept any actions when prompted by security dialog boxes to complete the process to allow the installer to make changes on your computer.

6. When the installation is complete, click **Finish**. You are ready to log in to your iCloud account.

> NOTE: **Requirements for iCloud**
> iCloud works with Microsoft Windows 7 or 8. You also need to install version 2.1.1 of the iCloud control panel and have iTunes 11 or later installed. To have your calendars and contacts synced via iCloud, you need to have Outlook 2007 or 2010 installed. To sync your bookmarks, you need to have either Safari version 5.1.7 or later or Internet Explorer 9 or later.

Logging In to Your iCloud Account

To start using iCloud, you need to log in to your iCloud account using the following steps:

1. Open the iCloud control panel, as shown in Figure 4.1.

FIGURE 4.1   To start using iCloud on your Windows PC, log in to your iCloud account.

2. Enter your Apple ID.

3. Enter your Apple ID password.

4. Click **Sign In**. You log in to your iCloud account, as shown in Figure 4.2. iCloud services become available, and you're ready to configure the specific services you want to use on the control panel, which now shows the services instead of the sign-in tools.

FIGURE 4.2   These settings enable or disable information syncing and services for your iCloud account.

Configuring and Managing Your iCloud Services

You can configure and manage the iCloud services you use by completing the following steps:

1. Open the iCloud control panel. As shown in Figure 4.3, in the right part of the pane, you see the iCloud services available on your Windows PC. If a service's check box is checked, that information (such as Mail, Contacts, Calendars, & Tasks with Outlook) is synced with the cloud or the service (such as Photo Stream) and is enabled on your computer. At the bottom of the pane, you see the iCloud Storage gauge and Manage button that enables you to work with your space on the cloud (more on this shortly). In the left part of the pane, you see the Apple ID currently logged in.

FIGURE 4.3   Use the iCloud pane to configure the services you use on your Windows PC.

NOTE: Outlook Assumed

Outlook is the dominant email, calendar, and task management application on Windows PCs and so this book is based on Outlook being installed. If you don't have Outlook installed on your Windows computer, your screens and the iCloud functionality available to you may be somewhat different than what is described in this book.

---

2. Check the **Show the iCloud status in Notification Area** check box if you want to be able to access the iCloud control panel or get iCloud help by clicking the iCloud icon in the Windows Notification Area located in the bottom-right corner of the desktop.

3. To include specific information in the sync process or to activate a service, check its check box, as shown in Figure 4.3; if you uncheck a check box, that information is removed from the sync process or the service is disabled.

   Some choices have an Options button you can click to make additional selections. Table 4.1 provides a list of the information or services you can select and shows you where to get more information about them.

TABLE 4.1 iCloud Options on a Windows PC

Information	Description	Where to Find More Information
Mail with Outlook	iCloud email	Lesson 9, "Configuring Your iCloud Email"
Contacts with Outlook	Contact information	Lesson 10, "Using iCloud to Manage Your Contacts"
Calendars & Tasks with Outlook	Calendars iCloud reminders and Outlook tasks	Lesson 11, "Using iCloud with Your Calendars" (calendars) Lesson 12, "Using iCloud to Sync Other Information" (tasks/reminders)
Bookmarks with Internet Explorer or Bookmarks with Safari	Safari or Internet Explorer bookmarks	Lesson 12, "Using iCloud to Sync Other Information"
Photo Stream	Photo storage in the cloud	Lesson 7, "Using iCloud with Your Photos"

Here are some other pointers to keep in mind as you work with the iCloud control panel:

▶ When you disable information syncing, you're prompted to keep or delete the iCloud information that is currently stored on your computer. If you select the **Keep** option, the sync process is stopped, but the information that has previously been synced remains on your computer. If you select the **Delete** option, the information from iCloud is removed from your computer.

▶ The gauge at the bottom of the pane shows your current storage space use. The more the bar is filled in, the less free space you have available to you on the cloud. Click the **Manage** button, and the Manage Storage dialog box appears, as shown in Figure 4.4. In the left pane of the window, you see the services and applications that are currently using your storage space and how much space each is using. When you select an application, you see the documents or data currently being stored for that application and how much space each item is consuming. If you select a service, such as **Backups**, you see how that service is using your iCloud storage space. Click **Done** to close the sheet.

TIP: **Freeing Space**

You can delete a document or other data by selecting it and clicking **Delete**. You can delete all the documents for an application by selecting the application and clicking **Delete All**. Of course, you don't want to do either of these unless you are sure you don't need the documents any more or you have them stored in a different location. If you previously backed up a device to your iCloud account but no longer need to do this, select **Backups**, click the device, and click **Delete**.

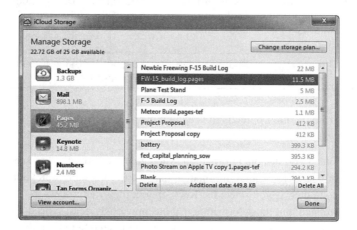

FIGURE 4.4   Here, you see how your iCloud storage space is being used.

▶ On the iCloud Storage dialog box, click **View account**, enter your account's password, and click **View account** again. The storage information is replaced by the Apple ID Summary dialog box. Here, you can change the storage plan for your account (click the upper **Change** button), edit your payment information (click the **Edit** button), or change the country or region associated with your account (click the lower **Change** button). Click **Done** when you are finished making changes.

▶ Click the **Change storage plan** button on the iCloud Storage dialog box, and you see the Buy More Storage dialog box, as shown in Figure 4.5. The highlighted amount with the check mark is your current plan. To upgrade the space available to you, click the option you want to select, click **Next**, and then follow the onscreen instructions to add more space to your account. If you upgraded your storage and decide you want to reduce it again, click the **Downgrade Options** button and follow the onscreen instructions to reduce the space allocated to your account.

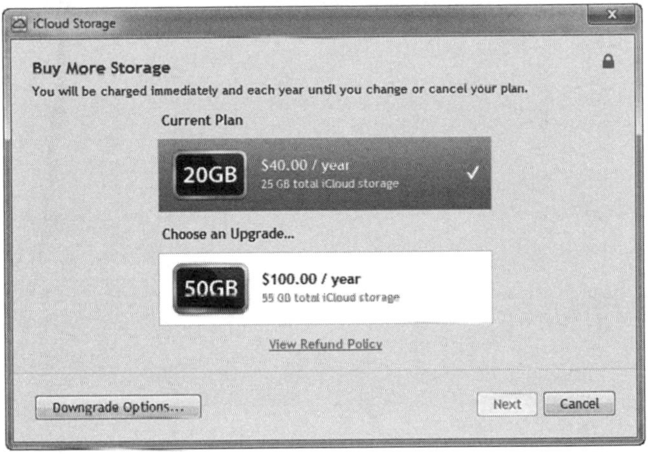

FIGURE 4.5 Use this dialog box to view your current storage plan or to upgrade or downgrade the amount of space available to you on the cloud.

▶ You can sign out of your iCloud account by clicking **Sign Out** on the iCloud control panel. You're prompted to keep or delete the iCloud information currently on your computer. After you make a choice, you are logged out of your iCloud account. The iCloud control panel returns to the state that allows you to sign in to your account. You can sign back in to your account or sign in to a different iCloud account.

NOTE: **One iCloud Account at a Time**

Although it's possible for you to have more than one iCloud account, you can only access one at a time for each user account on your computer.

Summary

In this lesson, you learned how to set up your iCloud account on a Windows computer. In the next lesson, you learn how to use iCloud for music, apps, and books.

LESSON 5

Using iCloud with iTunes Music, Apps, and Books

In this lesson, you learn how to use iCloud to make sure the music, apps, and books you purchase from the iTunes Store are always available to you on any device.

Understanding Automatic iTunes Store Purchase Downloading

The iTunes Store offers lots of great music, movies, TV shows, books, and so on, that you can purchase, download, and enjoy on iOS devices and computers. Before iCloud, to get the same media on more than one device, you had to use the sync process to move the content into iTunes on a computer (unless it was purchased on the computer, of course) and then use iTunes to sync that content onto other devices. And it was even more work to make your iTunes Library available on both a Mac and a PC.

iCloud takes away these hassles in a couple of ways. First, you can configure all your equipment (computers and iOS devices) to automatically download any future music, app, or book purchases you make from the iTunes Store. Second, you can easily download any past purchases of music, movies, TV shows, apps, or books directly onto your iOS devices.

Configuring your devices for automatic downloading is covered in a section for each type of device: iOS, Macs, and Windows PCs. You need to read only the sections that are relevant to the devices you use.

> NOTE: **Rented Instead of Purchased?**
>
> Movies you rent can only exist on one device at a time. If you didn't rent the movie on the device on which you want to watch it, you need to move it back to your iTunes Library and from there move it onto a different device through the sync process. In some cases, you can only watch a rented movie on the device you used to rent it, such as when you rent a movie on an iOS device or on Apple TV.

Using iCloud to Download iTunes Store Purchases on an iOS Device

An iCloud account helps you get content you purchased from the iTunes Store onto your iOS device with ease; this works for music, TV shows, apps, and books. In this section, you learn two ways to use iCloud to get purchased content on your iOS device:

- ▶ Add content you purchase in the future to all your devices automatically.

- ▶ Download previously purchased content.

> NOTE: **A Third Way**
>
> You can also use iTunes Match to stream music in your iTunes Library on an iOS device. This is explained in Lesson 6, "Using iTunes Match with Your Music."

Configuring Automatic Downloading of iTunes Store Purchases on an iOS Device

To configure automatic downloads to your iOS devices of the content you purchase from the iTunes Store, perform the following steps:

1. Tap **Settings**. The Settings app opens.

NOTE: Assumptions

The following steps are written with the assumption that you are logged in to the Apple ID you will use to purchase content from the iTunes Store. The account currently logged in is shown at the top of the iTunes & App Stores screen.

---

2. Tap **iTunes & App Stores**. You move to the iTunes & App Stores settings screen.

3. Set the **Music**, **Apps**, and **Books** switches to ON to have these types of content downloaded to your device automatically, as shown in Figure 5.1.

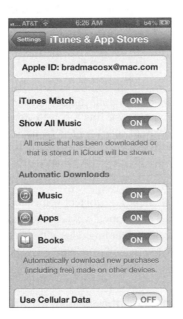

FIGURE 5.1   With this configuration, any music, apps, or books purchased from the iTunes Store on any iCloud-enabled device are automatically down-loaded to this iPhone.

4. If you are configuring a device that supports a cellular data connection (iPhone or iPad) and you don't have an unlimited data

plan, ensure that **Use Cellular Data** is OFF. Downloading music and other types of content can require significant amounts of data; if you have a limited data plan and go over your limit, this can get expensive. Therefore, you should set this to OFF so content is only downloaded when you are on a Wi-Fi network.

If **Use Cellular Data** is ON, content will be downloaded to your device when you use a cell network for data or when you are using a Wi-Fi network. If you have a data plan that doesn't limit the amount of data you can download, you can set this to ON. However, even in that case, some providers will slow down your Internet connection once you have downloaded a large amount of data during the current service period, so you may want to leave it set to OFF to ensure you don't reach this point in your data use.

TIP: **Apple ID**

At the top of the iTunes & App Stores screen, you see the Apple ID currently logged in. If you tap this, you see a menu with a number of useful commands. You can use this menu to view your Apple ID, sign out of your account, or reset your password. If you sign out of your account, the Store screen only has the Sign In button. Tap this and sign in to the Apple ID you want to use.

After you've done these steps, any content you enabled in step 3 is downloaded to the iOS device automatically when you purchase it from the iTunes Store on any device, including other iOS devices, Macs, and Windows PCs. (This only affects future purchases, but in the next section, you learn how to get previously purchased content.)

TIP: **Downloading TV Show Purchases**

Although you can't configure your device to automatically download TV show or movie purchases, you can easily download TV shows or movies you've downloaded from the iTunes Store in the past—as you learn in the next section.

Downloading Previous iTunes Store Music, TV Show, or Movie Purchases on an iOS Device

You can download music, movies, or TV shows you've previously purchased to an iOS device using the iTunes app. This works a bit different on an iPhone or iPod touch than it does on an iPad. See the section that applies to the device you are using.

> NOTE: **Technically Speaking**
>
> You really don't have to use iCloud to be able to manage your iTunes, App, and iBook Store purchases as described in this lesson. However, most people use the same Apple ID for iCloud and the various stores, so practically speaking, this functionality all comes through the same account (your Apple ID) even though, technically speaking, different sources are involved (iCloud versus the iTunes Store).

Downloading Previous iTunes Store Music, TV Show, or Movie Purchases on an iPhone or iPod touch

To download prior purchases on an iPhone or iPod touch, perform the following steps:

1. Open the **iTunes** app.

2. Tap the **More** button on the toolbar at the bottom of the screen.

3. Tap **Purchased**.

4. Tap the type of content you want to download; the options are **Music**, **Movies**, and **TV Shows**. The rest of these steps describe downloading music; downloading the other types of content is very similar.

5. Tap the **Not On This** *Device* tab, where *Device* is the type of device you are using, such as an iPhone or iPod touch. You see the list of artists whose music you have downloaded from the iTunes Store that isn't currently stored on the device. Next to each artist, you see how many songs are available for download

(see Figure 5.2). At the top of the list, you see the Recent Purchases selection, which takes you to the songs by any artist you've downloaded recently.

FIGURE 5.2   This list shows artists whose music I've downloaded from the iTunes Store but isn't currently stored on this iPhone.

6. Swipe up or down the list to find the artist whose songs you want to download.

TIP: **Recent Purchases**

To download recently purchased music, tap **Recent Purchases**. You see a list of up to 250 songs you have purchased recently, organized by the tabs at the top of the screen, which are **Most Recent**, **Name**, and **Artist Name**. Tap the tab to see the list organized by that option. You can swipe up or down the resulting list to find music you want to download.

---

7. Tap the artist whose music you want to download. You see the list of albums and music videos by that artist (see Figure 5.3). There are a number of ways you can download these songs.

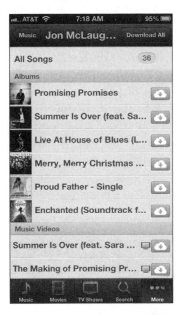

FIGURE 5.3   Here, I'm browsing music by Jon McLaughlin that isn't currently stored on my iPhone.

8. To download all of the artist's music, tap **Download All** and skip to step 15.

9. To download all of the songs on a specific album or a music video, tap its download button (the cloud with a downward-facing arrow) and skip to step 15.

10. To download songs on a specific album, tap the album. You see the list of songs on that album.

11. To download a song, tap its download button or to download all of the album's songs, tap the download button at the top of the screen; skip to step 15.

12. To download songs from any album, tap **All Songs**. You see the list of all the songs by the artist.

13. Tap **Most Recent** to see the songs list based on when you downloaded them or tap **Name** to see them listed by name.

14. To download a song, tap its download button.

15. To monitor the progress of the download, tap **More** and then tap **Downloads**. On the Downloads screen, you can see which songs you are downloading and where each is in the download process (see Figure 5.4). When the download process is finished, the song is stored on your device and is ready for you to enjoy. When all the songs have been downloaded, the screen becomes empty. This step is optional; the download process continues regardless of you viewing the Downloads screen. You can begin downloading music, and while it is downloading, you can select and download other music.

FIGURE 5.4 On the Downloads screen, you can see how your downloads are progressing.

> TIP: **Not So Fast**
>
> To halt the download process, tap the **Pause** button next to the content being downloaded. To start the download again, tap the **Resume** button (downward facing arrow).

Downloading Previous iTunes Store Music, TV Show, or Movie Purchases on an iPad

To download prior purchases on an iPad, perform the following steps:

1. Open the **iTunes** app.

2. Tap **Purchased** on the toolbar at the bottom of the screen.

3. Tap the type of content you want to download by tapping the related tab at the top of the screen; the options are **Music**, **Movies**, and **TV Shows**. The rest of these steps show downloading music; downloading the other types of content is very similar.

4. Tap **Not On This iPad**. Along the left side of the screen, you see the list of artists whose music you have downloaded from the iTunes Store that isn't currently stored on the device. At the top of the list, you see the Recent Purchases selection, which takes you to the songs by any artist you've downloaded recently.

5. Swipe up or down the list to find the artist whose songs you want to download or tap a letter or the # symbol on the index to jump to that section.

6. Tap the artist whose music you want to download. The list of songs by that artist appears in the right part of the screen (see Figure 5.5).

7. Tap the **Sort by** menu in the upper-right corner of the screen and choose **Songs by Most Recent**, **Songs by Name**, **Albums by Most Recent**, or **Albums by Name** to change how the content shown is sorted.

8. To download all of the songs by the artist, tap the **Download All** button at the top of the screen and skip to step 14.

FIGURE 5.5 Here, I'm browsing music by the band Switchfoot that isn't currently stored on this iPad.

9. In one of the song views, tap the download button (the cloud with the downward-facing arrow) next to the song you want to download and then skip to step 14.

10. In one of the album views, tap the album containing songs you want to download. You see the list of songs for that album (see Figure 5.6).

11. Browse the list of songs.

12. To download a song, tap its download button. To download all the songs on the album, tap the download button next to the album's art at the top of the screen.

13. When you finish downloading content from the album, tap the **Done** button located in the upper-left corner of the screen.

FIGURE 5.6   You can download individual songs on an album from this screen.

14. Tap **Downloads**. On the Downloads screen, you can see which songs you are downloading and where each is in the download process (see Figure 5.7). When the download process is finished, the song is stored on your device and is ready for you to enjoy. When all the songs have been downloaded, the screen becomes empty. This step is optional; the download process continues regardless of you viewing the Downloads screen. You can start downloading music, and while it is downloading, you can select and download other music.

TIP: **Not So Fast**

To halt the download process, tap the **Pause** button next to the content being downloaded. To start the download again, tap the **Resume** button (downward facing arrow).

FIGURE 5.7 On the Downloads screen, you can monitor the progress of the music you are downloading.

NOTE: **Free Is Purchased**

In the context of iTunes Store content, free stuff is treated like content you have to pay for. So, you use the same tools to download content whether it is free or has a purchase price.

Downloading Previous iBook Store Purchases on an iOS Device

You can download books you've previously purchased to an iOS device using the iBooks app:

1. Open the iBooks app.

2. Tap the **Store** button.

3. Tap **Purchased** on the toolbar at the bottom of the screen.

4. Tap **All** to see all your purchased books or tap **Not On This Device**, where *Device* is the name of the device you are using, to see books that haven't been downloaded yet (see Figure 5.8).

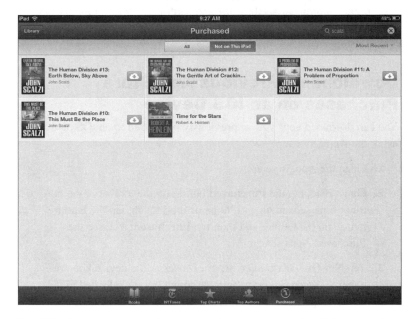

FIGURE 5.8   Here, you see books downloaded from the iBook Store that are not stored on the iPad—yet.

5. To download a book, tap its **Download** button (the cloud with the downward-facing arrow).

6. If prompted, enter your Apple ID password and tap **OK**. The book is downloaded to your device and becomes available in the library.

NOTE: **Downloaded Before?**

If a book was previously downloaded to the device but was removed through the sync process, it won't appear on the Not On This *Device* tab. To download it again, tap the All tab. Books that have been previously downloaded to the device but are not currently stored on it have the Download button. Tap this button to download the book to the device again.

> NOTE: **iCloud Is Optional Here, Too**
>
> As with music, TV shows, and movies, you can download books and apps you've purchased previously without being logged in to your iCloud account because they are associated with your iTunes/iBooks Store account.

Downloading Previous App Store Purchases on an iOS Device

You can download apps you've previously purchased to an iOS device using the App Store app:

1. Open the App Store app.

2. On an iPad, tap the **Purchased** button on the toolbar at the bottom of the screen; on an iPhone or iPod touch, tap the **Updates** button on the toolbar and then tap **Purchased**. You see the Purchased Apps screen.

3. Tap **Not On This** *Device*, where *Device* is the device you are using, to see apps you've purchased but not downloaded to the device. Figure 5.9 shows this screen on an iPad.

4. If you are using an iPad, open the menu located in the upper-right corner of the screen and tap **Most Recent** to see apps listed according to when you downloaded them or **Name** to see them listed by name.

5. Tap the **Download** button for the app you want to install on the device.

> NOTE: **Password or Not?**
>
> If you've entered your Apple ID recently, such as if you have just downloaded something, you won't have to enter again for a while. When the password isn't required, the content downloads to your device without it.

FIGURE 5.9   The Not On This iPad tab shows apps that have not been downloaded to this device.

6. If prompted, enter your Apple ID password and tap **OK**. The Download button is replaced by a status button that shows the app being installed on your device. When the installation process is complete, you can use the app.

NOTE: **Syncing and Purchased Content**

When you sync your iOS devices to iTunes, any purchased content is copied into your iTunes Library automatically.

Using iCloud to Automatically Download iTunes Store Purchases on a Mac

You can configure iTunes on a Mac to automatically download your music, app, and book purchases so they are stored in your iTunes Library. This is useful to store your content, and you can use iTunes to enjoy the content on your Mac. Here's how to make this happen:

1. In iTunes, choose **iTunes, Preferences**.

2. Click the **Store** tab.

3. Check the **Music**, **Apps**, and **Books** check boxes if you want these types of content downloaded to your Mac automatically, as shown in Figure 5.10; if you leave a check box unchecked, that type of content won't be downloaded automatically.

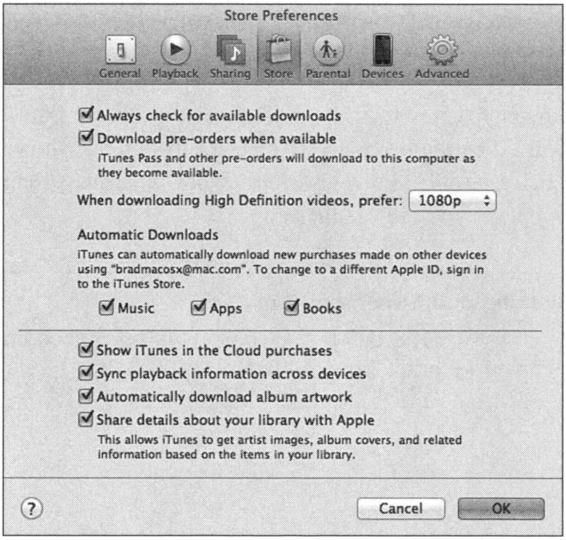

Figure 5.10   With these selections, music, apps, and books purchased on any device are automatically downloaded to this Mac.

4. Click **OK**. Any music, apps, or books you download from the iTunes Store are downloaded to your Mac automatically no matter which device you use to download them.

TIP: **Home Sharing**

Though not part of iCloud, it can be useful to stream content in your computer's iTunes Library to other computers, iOS devices, or Apple TVs through the Home Sharing feature in iTunes. Turn on **Home Sharing** through the **File** menu in iTunes and sign in to the account associated with the content you want to share.

To access shared content such as music on an iOS device, open the Music app, tap **More**, tap **Shared**, and tap the name of the library on which you enabled Home Sharing. You can browse and play the content in that library. You can watch shared video in the Videos app in the same way.

On an Apple TV, choose **Computers**, choose **Turn On Home Sharing**, and then enter the user name and password for the Home Share account. You can then watch or listen to content in the Home Share library.

On a computer, open iTunes and open the Source menu located in the upper-left corner of the window, just below the playback controls. Choose the Home Share library you want to access. The content of that library becomes available for you to enjoy (you need to sign in to the same home share via the File menu to be able to access that library).

TIP: **Downloading Previous Purchases on a Computer**

You can re-download prior purchases on a Mac or Windows PC by accessing the iTunes Store from within the iTunes application. Move to the content you want to re-download and download it using the same process as for content you haven't purchased—except for the paying-for-it part of course.

Using iCloud to Automatically Download iTunes Store Purchases on a Windows PC

You can configure iTunes on a Windows PC to automatically download your music, app, and book purchases so they are stored in your iTunes Library. This is useful to store your content, and you can use iTunes to enjoy the content on your computer. To enable automatic downloads, perform the following steps:

1. In iTunes, choose **Edit**, **Preferences**.

2. Click the **Store** tab.

3. Check the **Music**, **Apps**, and **Books** check boxes if you want these types of content downloaded to your computer automatically, as shown in Figure 5.11; if you leave a check box unchecked, that type of content won't be downloaded automatically.

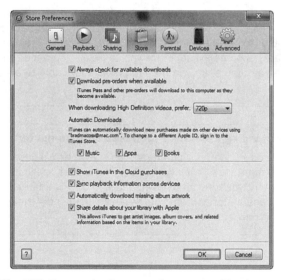

FIGURE 5.11   With these selections, music, apps, and books purchased on any device are downloaded automatically to this computer.

4. Click **OK**. Any music, apps, or books you download from the
iTunes Store are downloaded to your Windows PC automatically, no matter which device you use to download them.

TIP: **Yet Another Way to Share**

You can share content in your iTunes Library with other computers
on the same local network. Open iTunes Preferences. Click the
Sharing tab. Click the top check box to share your library and then
choose to share the entire library or only selected playlists. You can
also configure a password if you want.

You can access libraries being shared by clicking on them in the
SHARED LIBRARIES section of the iTunes Source menu. If required,
enter the password. You can then select the shared source and then
browse and play its content.

Summary

In this lesson, you learned how to use iCloud so that you have all your
music, app, and book purchases available on all your devices. In the next
lesson, you learn how to use iTunes Match to stream your music to your
iOS devices.

LESSON 6

Using iTunes Match with Your Music

In this lesson, you learn how to use iTunes Match to make your music available from the cloud so you can stream it to your iOS devices and computers.

Understanding iTunes Match

iTunes Match puts all of the music in your iTunes Library on the cloud so you can download and stream that music to your devices over the Internet. This makes your music available to you wherever you are (assuming you have an Internet connection in that location, of course). iTunes Match works for all the music in your Library, not just for music you've purchased from the iTunes Store (which, as you learned in Lesson 5, "Using iCloud with iTunes Music, Apps, and Books," you can download directly to any of your devices at any time). For example, if you've imported music from a CD into your library instead of buying that music in the iTunes Store, you can download it to your device just as easily as if you had purchased it in the iTunes Store. This eliminates the need to sync your music on your devices because you can access the music you want to hear at any point in time; you always see all the music in your iTunes Library on all the devices that are configured to use iTunes Match. If music you want to hear isn't currently stored on your device, you just tap the **Download** button to download it to your device, or you can tap a song to start the download process; when enough of the song has been downloaded, it will start to play too.

NOTE: **Match Account Not Computer**

It helps to realize that iTunes Match is tied to your Apple ID, not to a specific iTunes Library. If you enable iTunes Match on more than one computer, all the music from each computer is uploaded to the cloud, and each can download and play that music from the cloud.

There are a couple of points about this service that you need to be aware of. First, if you want to use iTunes Match, you must pay for the service; the cost is currently $24.99 per year in the United States (it may have a different price in other areas). The second point is trivial, but worth noting: If you configure an iOS device to use iTunes Match, the Music tab of the Sync screen contains only a check box to indicate if you want your voice memos synced. All your music is always available to you on your device, so there is no need to sync it.

NOTE: **Quality Counts**

iTunes Match music is delivered in the Advanced Audio Coding (AAC) format encoded at 256Kbps. If music in your iTunes Library is not already in this format, a temporary version in this format is created and then uploaded to the cloud. This format may actually be higher quality than the music that is permanently stored in your iTunes Library.

Whether or not you benefit from iTunes Match depends on your specific circumstances. If you only have music from the iTunes Store in your iTunes Library, you don't need iTunes Match because you can already download any purchased music to your device at any time for no additional cost. If your devices have enough space to store all the music in your iTunes Library along with all the other content you want, you don't really need iTunes Match because you can store all your music on the device anyway. If you have a lot of music from sources other than the iTunes Store in your library or if your iOS devices don't have enough space to store all the music in your library, iTunes Match may be right for you.

There are two basic steps to enabling iTunes Match. Step 1 is to activate iTunes Match in iTunes on a computer; this puts all your music in the cloud. Step 2 is to configure your devices to use iTunes Match.

After these two steps are done, you can listen to any of your music on your devices at any time.

> NOTE: **iTunes Match Caveats**
>
> iTunes Match uploads up to 25,000 songs, not counting those you have purchased from the iTunes Store. Song files over 200MB won't be uploaded to the cloud. Songs protected with Digital Rights Management (DRM) won't be uploaded unless your computer is authorized to play those songs.

Configuring and Managing iTunes Match in iTunes

To get started with iTunes Match, set it up in iTunes. This puts all your music on the cloud.

After you've configured iTunes to use iTunes Match, you can use its tools to manage your iTunes Match service.

Setting Up iTunes Match in iTunes

To start using iTunes Match, perform the following steps:

1. In iTunes, choose **Store**, **Turn On iTunes Match**. You move to the iTunes Match screen.

2. Click **Subscribe for $24.99 Per Year**.

3. Enter your Apple ID password (assuming your Apple ID is currently shown in the Apple ID field; if not, you need to sign out of the current account in the iTunes Store and sign in to the correct one).

4. Click **Subscribe**.

5. Follow the onscreen instructions to review or update your payment or other information, as required. iTunes Match starts the upload process, which has three steps. During step 1, iTunes collects information about your iTunes Library (see Figure 6.1). During step 2, iTunes matches songs in your iTunes Library with those available in the iTunes Store; these songs immediately become available to play on your devices.

FIGURE 6.1   iTunes Match is gathering information about the music in this iTunes Library.

During step 3, iTunes uploads songs in your library that aren't in the iTunes Store; this part of the process can take a while depending on the number of songs involved. You can use iTunes for other things during this process. You can check the progress at any time by selecting **Music Source** and clicking the **Match** button on the toolbar at the top of the screen. When the process is complete, you see how many songs are available to you in the cloud, as shown in Figure 6.2.

FIGURE 6.2 This screen shows you that the match process is complete, along with the number of songs available to you on the cloud.

NOTE: **More on Music Uploading**

All the music in your iTunes Library falls into one of two categories. One is that the music is available in the iTunes Store; any music that falls into this category is immediately available on the cloud whether you purchased it in the iTunes Store or not. The other is that the music is not available in the iTunes Store; in this situation, the music is uploaded to the cloud.

---

6. Click **Done**. Your music is in the cloud and ready for you to listen to it from any of your devices.

Managing iTunes Match in iTunes

Following are some tips to help you manage iTunes Match:

▶ If you add new music to your Library, such as importing a CD, you can refresh your music on the cloud by choosing **Store**,

Update iTunes Match. iTunes Match goes through the three-step process again, which adds any new music in your iTunes Library to the cloud.

▸ When iTunes Match is active, you see the cloud icon right below the Play button when you are viewing the Music in your library (Music is selected on the Source menu). When you work with the Music source in one of the views that show columns of information, such as the Songs list, you see a column with the cloud icon at the top, which indicates the iTunes Match status of the song.

When you don't see any icon in this column, it means the song is stored on the computer. A cloud with a downward-facing arrow indicates that the song is available on the cloud and can be played or downloaded. A cloud with a slash through it indicates the song isn't eligible for iTunes Match for some reason; for example, digital booklets that you get with some music can't be added to the cloud. A cloud with an exclamation point indicates that there was an error uploading the song; use the Update iTunes Match command on the Store menu to try to fix the problem. Two clouds with a slash through them indicate a duplicate; duplicates are not uploaded to the cloud.

▸ If you want to stop using iTunes Match, choose **Store**, **Turn Off iTunes Match**. Your music remains on the cloud, but the music in the iTunes Library is no longer matched.

▸ To re-enable iTunes Match, choose **Store**, **Turn On iTunes Match**. You move back to the iTunes Match screen. Click **Add This Computer**. iTunes Match goes through the three-step process of matching music again.

Listening to Your iTunes Match Music on an iOS Device

Before you can use iTunes Match on an iOS device, you need to configure the device to use iTunes Match as its source of music; you only have to do this once. After that is done, you can easily listen to any of your music on the iOS device.

Configuring an iOS Device to Use iTunes Match

Set up an iOS device to use iTunes Match by completing the following steps:

1. Tap **Settings**. The Settings app opens.

2. Tap **Music**.

3. Set the **iTunes Match** switch to ON.

4. Tap **Enable** at the prompt explaining that the music content on the device will be replaced.

5. If you want all the music available to you to be shown in the device, set the **Show All Music** switch to ON, as shown in Figure 6.3; if you set this to OFF, only music that has been downloaded to the device is shown. The music stored in the cloud is now available to the device.

NOTE: **Show All Music**

The Show All Music setting determines the music that is displayed in the Music app based on its iTunes Match status. When this is set to ON, you see all the music in the cloud, regardless of whether it has been downloaded to the device. This enables you to browse all your music. When it's set to OFF, only music that has previously been downloaded (and is now stored) on the device is shown. The OFF setting is useful for those times when you don't have an Internet connection available or if you want to avoid downloading music for a period of time (such as when you are roaming and want to ensure you don't use any more data than necessary). Most of the time, you'll probably want this to be ON so you can see and access all your music.

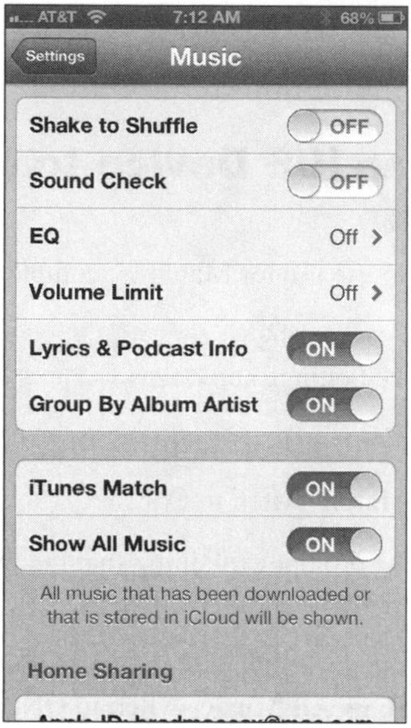

FIGURE 6.3   This iPhone is configured to get music from the cloud.

Listening to iTunes Match Music on an iOS Device

iTunes Match is so useful because you don't have to worry about syncing the music in your iTunes Library to your iOS devices; any music in your iTunes Library is available for your listening pleasure. If the music you want to hear isn't already stored on the device, when you select it, it gets downloaded and begins to play.

Listening to music with iTunes Match is very similar to listening to music that you've moved onto your device via the sync process. The difference is that you may have to download the music to your device before it starts to play.

Music that needs to be downloaded to your device is marked with the download icon (the cloud with a downward-facing arrow); if you don't see this icon, the music has already been downloaded, and you can listen to it immediately.

CAUTION: **Downloading Music via a Cellular Connection**

Music files are fairly large. If you have a device that uses a cellular data connection and there is a limit to how much data is included with your plan, you need to be careful with iTunes Match because you may exceed your data plan's limits, which can be quite expensive. To prevent iTunes Match music from being downloaded when you are using your cellular connection, move to the Settings app and tap **iTunes & App Stores**. On the iTunes & App Stores screen, set the **Use Cellular Data** switch to OFF. In this state, you need to be connected to a Wi-Fi network to be able to download and stream music to the device. This is less convenient, but you won't risk overcharges from downloading too much data.

When iTunes Match is set up on your iOS device, finding and playing music is pretty similar to when your music is stored on the device. Use the Music app to browse or search for music to which you want to listen. All of your music is in one of the two following states:

▶ If the music doesn't have the cloud icon, it is already on your device and you can use the app's tools to play it.

▶ If the music is marked with the cloud icon, as shown in Figure 6.4, tap the song to start the download process and play the music. When enough of the music has been downloaded so that it can play smoothly, it starts to play.

Here are some additional points to ponder when it comes to using iTunes Match on an iOS device:

▶ If you have a slow connection, it might take a moment for a song that is downloading to start playing after you tap it.

▶ If you just want to download a song and listen to it later, tap the **download icon** instead of the song. The download status wheel replaces the icon and shows the progress of the download. When the song has been downloaded, the icon disappears and the song is stored on your device.

▶ You can download entire albums, playlists, and other content by tapping the **download icon** that appears next to the album's or playlist's name or artwork (see Figure 6.4 for an example).

FIGURE 6.4 Two songs of this album are downloaded; one is currently playing (marked with the speaker icon). Songs marked with the download icon are available to download and play.

▶ Tap **Shuffle** at the top of your screens to have the Music app randomly download and play content from the source you're browsing.

▶ If content is grayed out and doesn't have the cloud icon next to it, it is not available in the cloud so you can't download and play it. This is likely because it just hasn't been uploaded by iTunes Match yet. If you come back to the content at a later time, it will probably be available.

Listening to Your iTunes Match Music on a Computer

You can also use iTunes Match to listen to music on a computer. Similar to an iOS device, there are two steps to the process. First, add the computer to iTunes Match (you have to do this only once). Second, download and listen to music from the cloud.

Adding a Computer to iTunes Match

To be able to access your cloud music from a computer, perform the following steps:

1. Choose **Store**, **Turn On iTunes Match**.

2. Click **Add This Computer**.

3. Enter your account's password (assuming the correct Apple ID is shown in the Apple ID field; if not, you need to log out of the current account in the iTunes Store and sign in to the correct one).

4. Click **Add This Computer**. iTunes starts the three-step iTunes Match process. Any music that is in the current computer's iTunes Library but isn't in the cloud is added to your music collection on the cloud. If this computer doesn't have much music stored on it, the process is completed fairly quickly.

5. When the process is completed, click **Done**, as shown in Figure 6.5. You're now ready to listen to music from the cloud.

TIP: **Add Music Anywhere**

If you have iTunes Match enabled on all your computers and automatic downloads enabled on all your computers and iOS devices, where you purchase or upload music is irrelevant because it is available automatically on all your devices. Whenever you import a CD into iTunes, use **Store**, **Update iTunes Match** to add that music to the cloud. (This is optional because iTunes periodically updates iTunes Match, but doing this ensures the new CD is available right away.)

Figure 6.5   iTunes on this Windows PC is connected to the cloud.

Listening to iTunes Match Music on a Computer

Listening to music from the cloud on a computer is a snap. When the computer is connected to iTunes Match, the cloud icon appears next to Music when that is selected on the Source menu, as shown in Figure 6.6.

In iTunes, browse music as you normally would. Do any of the following to listen to music:

▶ If songs, albums, or other items aren't marked with the download icon, they are stored on the computer already and are ready to play whether the computer is connected to the Internet or not.

▶ To play a song, album, playlist, and so on without downloading it, select and play the item as you normally would. The music plays via streaming from the Internet, but is not stored on the computer. The next time you play it, it plays via streaming again. The computer has to be connected to the Internet to stream music.

FIGURE 6.6 Songs without the cloud icon have been downloaded to the computer and are ready to play. Other songs are easy to download and play as well.

▶ To download songs, albums, playlists, or other musical content, click the related **download icon**. The content is downloaded to the computer and stored in the iTunes Library. You can then play it without being connected to the Internet.

Summary

In this lesson, you learned how to use iTunes Match to access the music in your iTunes Library on any iOS device or computer. In the next lesson, you learn how to use iCloud's Photo Stream.

LESSON 7

Using iCloud with Your Photos

In this lesson, you learn how to take advantage of iCloud's Photo Stream to automatically have all of your photos on multiple devices and to share photos.

Understanding Photo Stream

If you have more than one device with which you take, store, edit, or view photos, you'll probably find that Photo Stream is one of iCloud's most useful features. Photo Stream stores your photos in the cloud so that you can access them on any device. The great news is that this happens automatically; you don't have to worry about syncing your photos among your devices because Photo Stream handles this for you.

Each of your devices can add photos to your Photo Stream (sender) and download photos from the Photo Stream (receiver). (Note that an Apple TV can only receive photos from Photo Stream.) For example, you can take photos with an iPhone and they are automatically uploaded to the cloud through your iCloud account. Those photos are then automatically downloaded, via Photo Stream, to all your devices on which Photo Stream is enabled (see Figure 7.1). You don't have to sync any of the devices to work with your photos; Photo Stream brings photos to and receives photos from each device automatically.

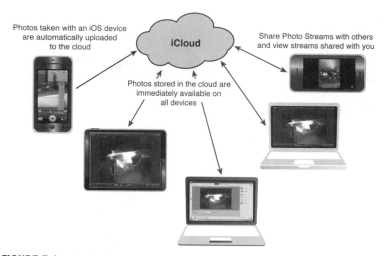

Photos taken with an iOS device are automatically uploaded to the cloud

iCloud

Share Photo Streams with others and view streams shared with you

Photos stored in the cloud are immediately available on all devices

FIGURE 7.1   Photo Stream eliminates the need to manually sync photos on your devices.

You can also use Photo Stream to share your photos with others. You designate the specific people with whom a particular collection of photos should be shared. Likewise, others can share their photos with you. Each shared Photo Stream includes the photos along with commentary; viewers can also indicate when they like photos in a shared stream. When new photos are added to a stream, the people sharing it are notified.

To use Photo Stream, you first configure it on each device. Once it is configured, how you work with your Photo Stream depends on the specific device you are using at the time. Throughout this lesson, you'll find sections devoted to working with Photo Stream on each type of device; you only need to read the sections that cover the devices you'll be using.

Following are some general points that will help you understand and use Photo Stream more effectively:

▶ When you take photos on an iOS device, they are uploaded to Photo Stream when you exit the Photos app and are connected to a Wi-Fi network (Photo Stream doesn't move photos over a cellular data connection). If you take photos while a device is not connected to a Wi-Fi network, they are uploaded the next time you connect it to a network.

▶ Photos are stored in your Photo Stream for 30 days.

▶ Because Photo Stream is not a long-term storage location, you need to make sure any photos you want to keep are stored in a permanent location if they aren't stored there automatically (photos you take with an iOS device are stored on that device).

▶ When photos are added to your Photo Stream and Photo Stream is enabled on a computer, the photos are downloaded onto your Mac (and stored in iPhoto '11 or Aperture 3.2) or Windows PC (and stored in the designated location) automatically. So, as long as you have a Mac or Windows PC set up to use Photo Stream, you don't have to worry about losing any of your photos.

▶ When you add photos to iPhoto or Aperture on a Mac or in the designated locations on a Windows PC, they are uploaded to your Photo Stream too.

▶ Your Photo Stream contains up to 1,000 photos. When you exceed that number, photos are removed from the Photo Stream automatically. If you don't also use Photo Stream with a Mac or a Windows PC, you should make sure the photos you want to keep from the Photo Stream are stored in a permanent location (this is explained later in this lesson).

▶ An Apple TV can only download photos from the Photo Stream.

▶ Photos are stored in your Photo Stream at their full resolution. They download to a Mac or Windows PC at the full resolution as well. When they are downloaded to an iOS device or an Apple TV, the resolution is optimized for the device.

▶ Photo Stream supports the most common photographic formats, such as JPEG, TIFF, PNG, and RAW. Photo formats only become a potential concern when you add photos to a Mac or Windows PC that weren't taken with an iOS device or a digital camera, such as images you download from the Internet. These images have to be in a supported format to be uploaded to your Photo Stream.

▶ Photos in your Photo Stream don't count against your iCloud storage space limit.

▶ Photo Stream doesn't support video. If you take videos with an iOS device, they only become available on other devices when you sync the device to a computer and then move the video onto other devices through the sync process or share it through a service, such as YouTube.

Using Photo Stream with iOS Devices

You could say that Photo Stream was designed with iOS devices in mind, and you'd be correct if you did. Photo Stream is an ideal way to make photos you take with one iOS device available on your other devices; it's also great because you can view and work with any of your photos on your iOS device as well. What's more, you can share your photos from an iOS device and work with photos other people share with you.

> NOTE: **iOS 6 Required**
>
> To make full use of Photo Stream, an iOS device must be running version 6 or later. You can use Photo Stream with iOS 5, but you won't be able to take advantage of photo sharing among other things.

To start using Photo Stream, enable it on each of your iOS devices. After Photo Stream is enabled, you don't need to do anything to upload photos you take with the device's camera to your cloud. This process happens automatically any time your device is connected to the Internet using a Wi-Fi network.

> NOTE: **Connect to Stream**
>
> An iPhone or iPad (with optional cellular capability) can use its cellular network or a Wi-Fi network, whereas an iPod touch uses a Wi-Fi network to connect to the Internet. However, Photo Stream only works over a Wi-Fi connection. Any photos you take on a device

while it isn't connected via Wi-Fi will be uploaded to the cloud as soon you connect to a Wi-Fi network. When you connect to a Wi-Fi network, any photos uploaded to the cloud since the device was last connected via Wi-Fi also become available on the device.

You can view and work with photos stored in your Photo Stream with the Photos app. This app enables you to view your Photo Stream photos, email them, tweet them, create Photo Streams to share, and so on. If you want to permanently store a photo contained in your Photo Stream on the iOS device, you can do that too.

NOTE: **Be Generous**
This part of the lesson describes and shows how to use Photo Stream on iOS devices, assuming photos are being shared. If you haven't shared any photos or aren't subscribed to shared Photo Streams, your screens may look a bit different. However, sharing Photo Streams is fun, so you should give it a try.

Enabling Photo Stream on an iOS Device

To start using Photo Stream on an iOS device, enable it with the following steps:

1. Open the Settings app.

2. Tap **iCloud**.

3. Tap **Photo Stream**.

4. Ensure that the **My Photo Stream** switch is in the ON position (see Figure 7.2). Your iOS device immediately accesses any photos available in your Photo Stream (assuming it is connected to the Internet via a Wi-Fi network, of course). Any photos you take with the device's camera after you enable Photo Stream are uploaded automatically (again, when the device is connected to the Internet via Wi-Fi).

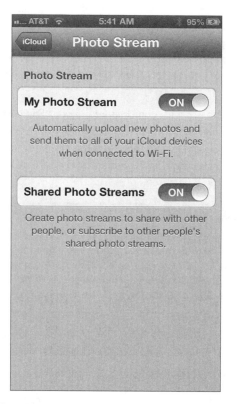

FIGURE 7.2   When Photo Stream is enabled, an iOS device automatically uploads captured photos to the cloud and downloads any photos stored there.

   5. To share your photos with others and access photos people share
   with you, ensure the **Shared Photo Streams** switch is set to ON.

TIP: **Another Way to Enable**

You can also enable Photo Stream by moving to the Settings app, tapping **Photos & Camera**, and ensuring the **My Photo Stream** and **Shared Photo Streams** switches are in the ON position.

Viewing Photo Stream Photos on an iOS Device

To view photos stored on your Photo Stream, perform the following steps (which are based on an iPad; iPhone or iPod touch screens look a bit different, but work in the same way):

1. Tap the **Photos** icon on the Home screen. The app opens.

2. Tap the **Photo Stream** tab.

3. Tap **My Photo Stream**.

4. Browse the photos stored in your Photo Stream. This works just like browsing photos in other albums on your device. You can drag your finger up or down the screen to scroll all the photos contained there.

5. To view a photo, tap its thumbnail. The photo appears on the photo viewer screen, as shown in Figure 7.3.

FIGURE 7.3 Viewing a photo from the Photo Stream is just like viewing photos you've take with an iOS device's camera.

Working with Photo Stream Photos on an iOS Device

When you tap the Action button (upper-right corner of an iPad screen or lower-left corner on an iPhone or iPod touch), you can perform the following actions with photos stored in your Photo Stream:

> TIP: **Swipe It**
>
> To see all of the options described in this list, you need to swipe to the left or right on the Action menu.

- ▶ **Mail**—Prepares a new email message with the photo attached.

- ▶ **Message**—Sends the photo to the Messages app where it is attached to a new message that you can send via iMessages or as a text message.

- ▶ **Photo Stream**—Copies the photo to a different Photo Stream.

- ▶ **Assign to Contact**—Associates the photo with a contact.

- ▶ **Use as Wallpaper**—Sets the photo as the wallpaper for your Home screen, the Locked screen, or in both locations.

- ▶ **Facebook**—Shares the photo via Facebook.

- ▶ **Twitter**—Sends the photo via Twitter.

- ▶ **Print**—Prints the photo on an AirPrint-capable printer.

> TIP: **Multiple Photos**
>
> You can perform some of these actions, such as emailing, messaging, or copying, on multiple photos at the same time. When you are browsing the Photo Stream album, tap the **Edit** button and then tap each photo you want to select. Tap the **Share** button. Then tap the command you want to use, and it will be performed on all the selected photos at the same time. For example, if you tap **Mail**, the photos you selected are attached to an email message.

► **Copy**—Copies the photo to the Clipboard so you can paste it into other apps.

► **Save to Camera Roll**—Saves the photo in the Camera Roll album. This causes the photo to be permanently stored on your iOS device rather than just being stored in your Photo Stream, which is not a permanent location (see the section, "Understanding Photo Stream," earlier in this lesson for details). (Photos you take with an iOS device are stored in the Camera Roll album, where they remain until you sync them to a computer, at which point you can choose to remove them from the device.)

Saving Photo Stream Photos on an iOS Device

If you don't use Photo Stream with a Mac or a PC or you want to store a photo from your Photo Stream on an iOS that wasn't used to take that photo, you need to store any photos in your Photo Stream that you want to keep in a permanent album. You can do this by saving them to the Camera Roll album or by creating an album on the iOS device and saving the photos there.

To create an album on an iOS device and save Photo Stream photos in it, perform the following steps:

1. Open the Photos app.

2. Tap the **Albums** tab.

3. Tap the **Add** (+) button.

4. Type the name of the album you are creating and tap **Save**, as shown in Figure 7.4. You're prompted to add photos to the new album.

5. Tap the **Photo Stream** tab.

6. Tap **My Photo Stream**.

7. Browse the photos in the Photo Stream.

FIGURE 7.4   You can create a photo album on an iOS device and store photos from your Photo Stream there.

8. Tap the photos you want to save in the new album. Photos you tap are marked with a check mark to show that they are selected, as shown in Figure 7.5.

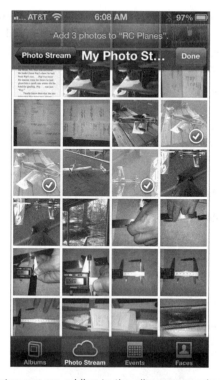

FIGURE 7.5   Photos you are adding to the album are marked with a check mark.

TIP: **Save Them All**

If you use an iPad and want to save all the photos in your Photo Stream in the new album, tap **Select All Photos** and skip steps 7 through 8.

9. Tap **Done**. The new album is created and the photos you selected are stored in it. You can work with the new album just like others you have on your device, and the photos it contains are permanently stored there.

To store photos from your Photo Stream in an album that already exists (such as the one you created with the previous steps), perform the following steps:

1. Open the Photos app.

2. Tap the **Photo Stream** tab.

3. Tap **My Photo Stream**.

4. Tap **Edit**.

5. Browse the photos in the Photo Stream.

6. Tap the photos you want to save in an album. Photos you tap are marked with a check mark to show that they are selected. As you tap photos, the number of photos you have selected is shown at the top of the screen.

7. Tap **Save**. You're prompted to choose an existing album or to create a new album and add the selected photos to it (this works similarly to the previous set of steps).

8. Tap **Save to Existing Album**. You move to the Albums tab, where you see all the albums in the Photos app. Albums you created on the device are highlighted, whereas albums coming from other sources are grayed out (this is more visible on iPads than on iPhones/iPod touches). This is because you can only copy photos to albums created on the device. The number of photos you are copying along with a thumbnail are shown at the top of the screen, as shown in Figure 7.6.

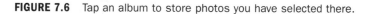

FIGURE 7.6   Tap an album to store photos you have selected there.

9. Tap the album in which you want to store the photos. The selected photos are stored in the album and you return to your Photo Stream. The photos you place in an album remain there even after they disappear from the Photo Stream.

Using Photo Stream to Share Photos on an iOS Device

To create a new, shared Photo Stream, do the following:

1. View a source of photos you want to share via Photo Stream.

2. Tap **Edit**.

3. Tap the photos you want to share.

4. Tap **Share**.

5. Tap **Photo Stream**; if this is the first Photo Stream you have shared, skip to step 7.

6. Tap **New Photo Stream**.

7. Enter the email addresses of the people with whom you want to share the photos.

8. Give the Photo Stream a name.

9. To make the photos available to anyone on iCloud.com, set the **Public Website** switch to ON (see Figure 7.7).

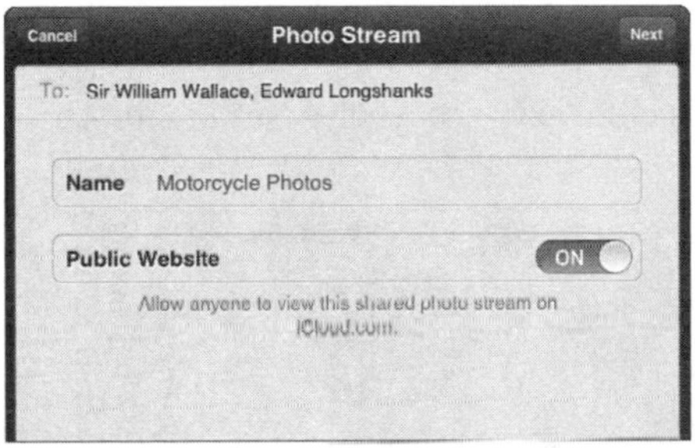

FIGURE 7.7 You can easily share photos on an iOS device by creating a shared Photo Stream.

10. Tap **Next**.

11. Add commentary about the Photo Stream you are sharing. You can add any text you want, such as a description of the photos you are sharing.

12. Tap **Post**. The Photo Stream is shared and the people with whom you shared it receive a notification (see the following section).

To add photos to an existing, shared Photo Stream, perform the previous task's steps, except in step 6, tap a shared Photo Stream instead of creating a new one. Enter your commentary and post the new photos. The photos are added to your shared Photo Stream and the people with whom you are sharing it receive notifications that new photos have been added to the stream to which they are subscribed.

To create a new, empty shared Photo Stream, tap the **Add** (+) button on the Photo Stream screen. Enter the information to share the Photo Stream and tap **Create**. The Photo Stream is created, although it doesn't contain any photos. You can add photos to the new stream as described in the previous paragraph.

Using Photo Streams Shared with You on an iOS Device

You can work with Photo Streams people are sharing with you, as follows:

1. Open the notification you receive (see Figure 7.8).

FIGURE 7.8   When someone shares a Photo Stream with you, you receive a notification like this.

2. Tap **Accept**. This moves you to the Photos app where you see the photos in the Photo Stream being shared with you.

3. View the photos using the same steps you use to view photos stored on your iOS device.

4. To see commentary about the photo, tap the **Quote** button (see Figure 7.9), which also indicates how many comments there are.

FIGURE 7.9   You can add commentary to photos being shared with you.

5. Tap **Add a comment** to add your own commentary to the photo.

6. Tap **Like** to indicate you like the photo.

When photos are added to the shared stream, you receive a notification informing you this happened. You can view and work with the new photos in the same way as those shared initially.

TIP: **Working with Shared Photos**

You can perform most of the same tasks with shared photos that you can with your own photos, such as emailing them, using them as wallpaper, and so on. To save a shared photo on your iOS device, tap the **Action** button and then tap **Save to Camera Roll**.

To unsubscribe from a Photo Stream on an iPad, open the **Photo Stream** tab and tap **Edit.** Double-tap the stream from which you want to unsubscribe. To unsubscribe from a Photo Stream on an iPhone/iPod touch, open the **Photo Stream** tab and tap the shared stream's **Info** button (right-facing arrow). On the Photo Stream's screen, you see the owner of the stream along with other people sharing it. Tap **Unsubscribe** and confirm that is what you want to do. The shared Photo Stream is removed from your iOS device.

Using Photo Stream with a Mac

Photo Stream works great with a Mac. Like with other devices, you need to first enable Photo Stream on the Mac. Then, you can work with your Photo Stream photos in either iPhoto or Aperture. Both applications automatically download and save all your Photo Stream photos, and of course you can edit them, save them in albums, use them in projects, and all the other great tasks you can do with any of your other photos stored in those applications.

NOTE: **Mac Requirements**

To use all of iCloud's functionality on a Mac, you must be running OS X, version 10.8.2 or later, along with iTunes 11 or later. To use Photo Stream, you need to have iPhoto '11, version 9.4 or later, or Aperture, version 3.4 or later.

Enabling Photo Stream on a Mac

To enable Photo Stream on a Mac, perform the following steps:

1. Open the System Preferences application.

2. Click **iCloud**. The iCloud pane appears.

3. Check the **Photo Stream** check box.

4. Click **Options**.

5. Ensure the **My Photo Stream** and the **Shared Photo Streams** check boxes are checked, as shown in Figure 7.10.

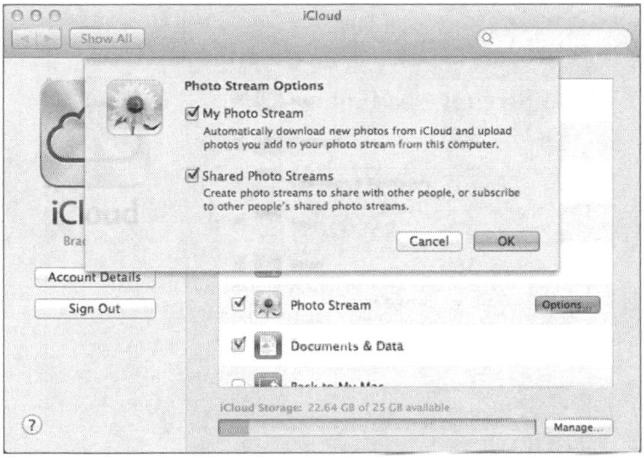

FIGURE 7.10   Enabling Photo Stream on a Mac requires just a few clicks.

6. Click **OK**. Photo Stream becomes available in iPhoto or Aperture and is ready to use in those applications.

TIP: **Importing Photos**
Neither iPhoto nor Aperture imports photos from your Photo Stream unless they are open. You should periodically open the applications to ensure your Photo Stream photos are downloaded. You need to do this at least every 30 days, and more frequently if you add more than 1,000 photos to your Photo Stream in less time.

Using Photo Stream with iPhoto

iPhoto enables you to work with your own photos by automatically downloading photos from your Photo Stream to your iPhoto Library and uploading any photos you add to iPhoto to the Photo Stream. You can also create shared Photo Streams and work with Photo Streams being shared with you.

Enabling iPhoto to Use Photo Stream

To get started, enable iPhoto to access your Photo Stream by performing the following steps:

1. Launch iPhoto.

2. Choose **iPhoto**, **Preferences**.

3. Click **Photo Stream** (see Figure 7.11).

FIGURE 7.11   In iPhoto, enable Photo Stream to connect the iPhoto Library to the cloud so you can share your photos.

4. Ensure the **My Photo Stream** check box is checked. This causes iPhoto to access your Photo Stream.

5. Ensure the **Automatic Import** check box is checked. This configures iPhoto to automatically download photos from your Photo Stream and add them to your iPhoto Library.

6. Ensure the **Automatic Upload** check box is checked. This causes iPhoto to automatically upload photos that you manually add to your iPhoto Library (such as by importing them from a digital camera) to your Photo Stream.

7. Ensure the **Shared Photo Streams** check box is checked. This enables you to share your photos and to work with photos being shared with you.

8. Close the Preferences dialog box.

iPhoto starts Photo Stream and downloads the photos currently stored there. Photos added there over time are automatically downloaded as well. When you add photos to iPhoto from other sources, such as importing them from a digital camera, they are uploaded to Photo Stream too.

Working with Your Photo Stream in iPhoto

As you work with Photo Stream and iPhoto, keep the following points in mind:

▶ You don't have to move photos from the Photo Stream to your iPhoto Library to store them on your Mac. This happens automatically when iPhoto downloads photos from the Photo Stream. You can view the Photo Stream photos stored on your Mac by selecting Photos or any of the other sources in the Library. After they are downloaded from Photo Stream, you can use all of iPhoto's tools on them, just like photos you've added from other sources (such as a digital camera).

▶ If there are a lot of photos in your Photo Stream when you first enable it in iPhoto, it can take a while for all of the photos to be downloaded to your Mac.

▶ To see the photos in your Photo Stream, select it on the Source list, as shown in Figure 7.12. The Photo Stream screen has two sections. In My Photos, you see the photos in your Photo Stream along with the streams you are sharing. In the Family and Friends' Photos section, you see streams being shared with you. You can browse and view the photos here just like other sources. For example, to see the photos in your Photo Stream, double-click **My Photo Stream** (because these photos are downloaded to your Mac automatically, you can also view them using the options in the Library, such as Events and Places). You can browse the photos in your Photo Stream, view them, and so on.

FIGURE 7.12 When you select the Photo Stream source, you see your Photo Stream along with photos you are sharing and those being shared with you.

▶ iPhoto periodically and automatically updates the Photo Stream source. While this is happening, you see the updating icon (a rotating circle made up of two curved arrows) next to the Photo Stream icon on the Source list. iPhoto updates the Photo Stream each time you launch the application.

Sharing Photo Streams in iPhoto

Photo Streams are great for sharing your photos with others. Anyone who uses iCloud and has Photo Stream enabled on a device (Mac, Windows PC, or iOS) can view your photos, add commentary, and so on, within the related app on their device (such as the Photos app on an iOS device).

You can create and share a new Photo Stream by performing the following steps:

1. Select the photos you want to share.

2. Click the **Share** button.

3. Choose **Photo Stream**.

4. Click **New Photo Stream**.

5. Enter the email addresses of the people with whom you want to share the photos.

6. Name the photo stream.

7. Check the **Public Website** check box if you want anyone to be able to view the photos using a web browser.

8. Click **Share** (see Figure 7.13). The new Photo Stream is created and the people with whom you are sharing it receive a notification that enables them to access it (see the next section for details).

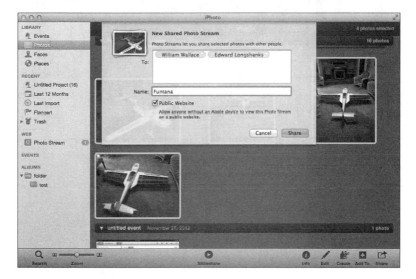

FIGURE 7.13 Creating a new Photo Stream to share just requires you to complete this dialog box.

When you select the Photo Stream source on iPhoto's Source list, you see the Photo Streams you are sharing in the My Photos section (see Figure 7.14). For each shared stream, you see a thumbnail of a photo in the stream, the stream's name, and how many people the stream is shared with or the name or email address of the person it is shared with (if it is only shared with one person).

FIGURE 7.14   I have shared four Photo Streams: Motorcycle Photos, Great Photos, Funtana RC Plane, and Photos for Ed.

You can add photos to an existing stream by doing the following:

1. Select the photos you want to add to an existing stream.

2. Click **Add To**.

3. Select **Photo Stream**.

4. Click the Photo Stream to which you want to add the photos.

5. If you selected a single photo in step 1, add a comment that you want to go along with the photo in the stream and then click **Publish**; if you selected more than one photo is step 1, you aren't prompted to add commentary (you can add it to individual photos later).

   The photos are added to the Photo Stream. The people with whom you are sharing the stream receive a notification that new photos have been added.

Following are some additional points to consider as you work with your shared Photo Streams:

▶ **Comments/Like**—People who can view your shared Photo Streams can add comments to them and indicate that they like them. You receive notifications when this happens, and the shared Photo Stream is marked with a blue circle. To see the comments, open the shared Photo Stream by double-clicking it. Photos with unread commentary are marked with a blue quote bubble; once you have read the commentary, the quote bubble is shown, but it is white instead. Click the photo to see the commentary along with information about who posted it and when. You also see who has liked the photo (see Figure 7.15).

FIGURE 7.15   Here you see that William Wallace likes this photo and has added commentary to it.

▶ **Converse**—Select a photo to share your own comments about it; then click **Add a comment**, type your comments, and click **Post**. Others who are sharing the stream receive notifications and can read your comments, enabling conversations about specific photos.

▶ **Get information**—To get information about a shared Photo
  Stream, select the stream and click the **Info** button on the toolbar. The Info pane opens (see Figure 7.16). Here, you can add a
  description, see who you are sharing the Photo Stream with and
  whether they have accepted it (check mark by the name instead
  of a question mark), turn Public Website sharing on or off, and
  visit the stream's website. You can remove a subscriber or
  resend the invitation by performing a secondary click on a person's name and choosing the action you want on the resulting
  menu.

FIGURE 7.16   On the Info pane, you can see information about a shared
Photo Stream.

▶ **Preview photos**—Move the pointer across a stream's thumbnail
  to preview the photos it contains.

▶ **Change the stream's name**—Select the name, edit it, and press
  Return to save the new name.

> NOTE: **Secondary Click**
>
> A secondary click is sometimes known as a right-click. There are a number of ways to do this. You can hold the Ctrl key down while you click, use a two-fingered gesture on a trackpad, click the right button on a mouse, and so on. The Ctrl+click option always works.

▶ **Remove a shared stream**—To delete a shared Photo Stream, perform a secondary click on it and choose **Delete Photo Stream**. When you delete a shared Photo Stream, it is no longer available to those who are subscribed to it. The photos remain in your iPhoto Library.

Working with Photo Streams Shared with You in iPhoto

When someone shares a Photo Stream with you, you see a notification, receive an email, and see the badge on the Photo Stream icon indicating you have new activity. To accept the shared stream in iPhoto, follow these steps:

1. Click **Photo Stream** in the WEB section on the iPhoto Source List. You see the new Photo Stream. You don't see a preview in the thumbnail since you haven't subscribed to it yet.

> TIP: **Show Me!**
>
> You can also click the **Show Me** button in the notification you receive or the **Join this Photo Stream** button in the notification email instead of performing step 1.

2. Hover over the Photo Stream's name. You see the Decline and Accept buttons.

3. Click **Accept** (see Figure 7.17). The subscription is added and you can work with the shared Photo Stream.

FIGURE 7.17 When you click the Accept button, you are subscribed to a Photo Stream.

> TIP: You can configure the notifications about shared Photo Streams by opening the Notifications pane of the System Preferences application and clicking **Photo Stream**.

Here are some things you can do with a shared Photo Stream to which you have subscribed:

▶ **Preview photos**—Move the pointer across the stream's thumbnail to preview the photos it contains.

▶ **Browse and view its photos**—Double-click a shared stream to see the photos it contains. You can browse and view these photos just like those stored in your iPhoto Library.

▶ **Import photos to your iPhoto Library**—Select the shared stream or open it and select the photos you want to add to your library, perform a secondary click, and then choose **Import**. The photos are downloaded and become part of your iPhoto Library.

▶ **Comment/Like**—Click the **Quote** button in the lower-left corner of the photo on which you want to comment. The Info pane opens. Enter your comments and click **Post**. Click **Like** to indicate you like the photo.

▶ **Remove a shared stream**—To get rid of a shared stream, perform a secondary click on it and choose **Unsubscribe**.

NOTE: **One Application at a Time**

You can use Photo Stream in only one application at a time. If you are already using Photo Stream in iPhoto and you try to use it in Aperture (or vice versa), you're prompted to change the application that accesses your Photo Stream. Also, photos are only downloaded from Photo Stream once. If you have downloaded all your Photo Stream photos into one application (such as iPhoto) and then switch to the other one (namely Aperture), only photos added to your Photo Stream after you make the switch are automatically downloaded to the current application.

Using Photo Stream with Aperture

Apple's Aperture photo application also supports Photo Stream. It automatically downloads photos from your Photo Stream and uploads photos you add to your Aperture Library from other sources, such as a camera.

Like with iPhoto, you need to enable your Photo Stream in Aperture:

1. Launch Aperture.

2. Choose **Aperture**, **Preferences**.

3. Click **Photo Stream** (see Figure 7.18).

4. Ensure the **My Photo Stream** check box is checked. This causes Aperture to access your Photo Stream.

5. Ensure the **Automatic Import** check box is checked. This configures Aperture to automatically download photos from your Photo Stream and add them to your Aperture Library.

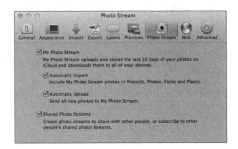

FIGURE 7.18   In Aperture, enable Photo Stream to connect the Aperture Library to the cloud to share your photos.

6. Ensure the **Automatic Upload** check box is checked. This causes Aperture to automatically upload photos you add to your Aperture Library (such as by importing them from a digital camera) to your Photo Stream.

7. Ensure the **Shared Photo Streams** check box is checked. This enables you to share your photos and to work with photos being shared with you.

8. Close the Preferences dialog.

    Aperture starts Photo Stream and downloads the photos currently stored there. Photos added there over time are automatically downloaded as well. When you add photos to Aperture from other sources, such as importing them from a digital camera, they are uploaded to Photo Stream too.

After Photo Stream is enabled, you can select it on the Source list to view the photos there, as shown in Figure 7.19. Like with iPhoto, because the Photo Stream photos are automatically stored in your library, you can work with them there rather than in the Photo Stream, but you can always see what's currently in your Photo Stream if that is of interest to you.

Also like iPhoto, the Photo Stream source has two sections. My Photos contains My Photo Stream, which is your Photo Stream, and the Photo Streams you are sharing with others. The Family and Friends section shows the Photo Streams that are being shared with you.

FIGURE 7.19 When you select Photo Stream in Aperture, you see the photos in your Photo Stream.

You can do the same tasks in Aperture that you can in iPhoto, though the interface is a bit different. Due to page limitations, it is not possible to include all the details in this section. However, showing you how to add photos to an existing shared Photo Stream should help you understand how to apply the information in the iPhoto section to Aperture:

1. Select the photos you want to add to a shared Photo Stream.

2. Click the **Share** menu on the toolbar.

3. Choose **Photo Stream**. The Photo Stream sheet appears.

4. On the Photo Stream menu, choose the Photo Stream to which you want to add the selected photos (see Figure 7.20).

TIP: **Create a New Shared Stream**

To create a new shared stream, choose **New Photo Stream** on the Photo Stream menu in step 4. Enter the email addresses of the people with whom you want to share the stream, give the stream a name, indicate if you want the photos to be public, and then click **OK**.

FIGURE 7.20 You can add photos to a shared stream with just a few mouse clicks.

5. Click **OK**. The photos are added to the shared stream, and the people subscribed to it receive a notification.

You can perform the other shared Photo Stream tasks, such as viewing streams being shared with you in Aperture, too; you just need to use the equivalent commands, menu options, and other user interface elements, which are somewhat different in Aperture than in iPhoto.

TIP: **Downloading Manually**

You can manually download photos from your Photo Stream into either iPhoto or Aperture. Just select and browse the Photo Stream source. Drag photos from that source onto the library. The downloaded photos are added to the library. You can re-download photos as many times as you'd like while they remain in your Photo Stream.

> CAUTION: **Photo Stream and Disk Space**
>
> As you've learned, when you use Photo Stream with a Mac or a Windows PC, photos are automatically downloaded and stored on your computer. You save time because manual syncing is not required. However, it also means that *every* photo you take with Photo Stream–enabled devices is permanently stored on your computer. If you take a lot of photos, this can consume a large amount of disk space. You should establish a habit of regularly "pruning" the photos downloaded from Photo Stream to your computer to remove photos you don't want to keep. You should also use your photo application to tag downloaded photos so that you can keep them organized and easy to find.

Using Photo Stream with a Windows PC

When you use Photo Stream with a Windows PC, photos are automatically downloaded to a folder you designate and uploaded from a folder you select. You can also share photos with others and work with photos being shared with you.

Like other devices, you first enable Photo Stream and then you can take advantage of the automatic photo downloads and uploads and the photo sharing that Photo Stream provides.

> NOTE: **Windows PC Requirements**
>
> iCloud works with Microsoft Windows 7 or 8. You also need to install version 2.1.1 of the iCloud control panel and have iTunes 11 or later installed. (The information in this section is based on Windows 7.)

Enabling Photo Stream on a Windows PC

To start using Photo Stream on a Windows PC, enable it with the following steps:

1. Open the iCloud control panel.

2. Check the **Photo Stream** check box.

3. Click **Options**. The Photo Stream Options dialog appears.

4. Ensure the **My Photo Stream** check box is checked.

5. Ensure the **Share Photo Streams** check box is checked.

6. If you want to change the location where Photo Stream photos are stored, check the **Change** button; in most cases, the default locations are fine and you can skip to step 9.

7. Move to and select the folder in which you want Photo Stream photos to be automatically downloaded and where you want to place photos to be uploaded automatically and then click **OK**.

8. Click **OK**.

9. Click **Apply**. Any changes you made are implemented.

Using Photo Stream Photos on a Windows PC

After you configure Photo Stream on your Windows PC, you can access its photos by opening the Photo Stream folder within your Pictures folder (unless you changed its location in the iCloud control panel), as shown in Figure 7.21.

In this folder, you see the following three subfolders:

▶ **My Photo Stream**—This folder contains all the photos currently in your Photo Stream. When you open it, you see the photos organized according to the current option, such as by Month or Folder. You can browse and view these photos using the standard Windows tools. You can also open and use them in a photo application, such as Adobe Photoshop Elements.

▶ **Shared**—This folder contains Photo Streams you are sharing and those being shared with you. When you open the folder, you see each shared Photo Stream (see Figure 7.22). You can open any of these folders to work with the photos it contains.

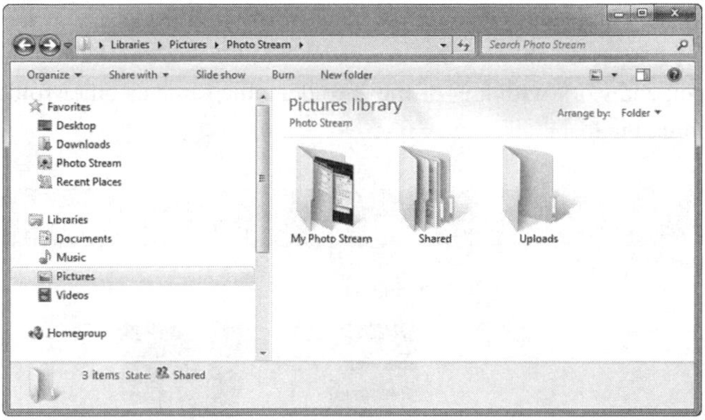

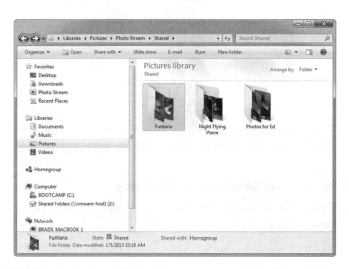

FIGURE 7.21   When you open the Photo Stream folder, you see the three subfolders shown here.

FIGURE 7.22   Each shared Photo Stream appears in the Shared folder.

▶ **Uploads**—Place photos in this folder that you want to upload to your Photo Stream.

You can also access your Photo Stream and shared streams by clicking **Photo Stream** in the Windows Favorites section. The resulting folder displays your Photo Stream along with those you are sharing and that are being shared with you (see Figure 7.23). For shared folders, you see the name of the person sharing the stream or "Me" if you are sharing it. You can open and work with any of these folders, the same as other folders containing photos.

FIGURE 7.23   Each shared Photo Stream appears in the Shared folder.

Sharing Photo Streams in Windows

You can share the photos in your Photo Stream with others by performing the following steps:

1. In My Computer, under Favorites, select **Photo Stream**.

2. Click **New Photo Stream** on the toolbar at the top of the window.

3. Click in the **To** field and enter the email addresses of the people with whom you want to share the photos.

4. Enter the name of the shared stream.

5. Check the **Create a public website to allow anyone to view this Photo Stream on icloud.com** check box if you want the photos to be publicly available on the Web.

6. Click **Next**, as shown in Figure 7.24.

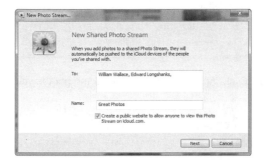

FIGURE 7.24 You can share photos from the Windows desktop by creating a new Photo Stream.

TIP: **Another Way to Share**

You can also create a new shared stream by selecting the photos you want to share, performing a right-click, choosing **Add to a Photo Stream**, and then clicking **New Photo Stream**. The dialog box shown in Figure 7.24 opens.

---

7. Click **Choose Photos**.

8. Use the resulting dialog box to move to and select the photos you want to share and then click **Open**. The photos are added to the dialog box, along with space to add comments.

NOTE: **Be Generous**

You can share any photos on your PC. If they aren't already on your Photo Stream, simply upload and then share.

---

9. Click **Add a Comment** and type a comment for each photo (see Figure 7.25).

FIGURE 7.25   Click "Add a comment" next to the photos you want to comment on.

10. Repeat steps 7 through 9 until you've added all the photos you want to share.

11. Click **Done**. The Photo Stream is created and shared. Your invitees receive notifications (Macs and iOS devices) and emails (Window PCs, Macs, and iOS devices). You see the new, shared stream in your Photo Stream folder.

People with whom you shared the stream can view, use, and comment on or like your photos on their devices. When activity happens, such as someone accepting a stream you are sharing, you see a notification on the Windows desktop.

When a stream has new activity, it is marked with the blue dot icon. Open the stream. Any photos with new activity are marked with the blue quote bubble. Click the quote bubble or click the **Comments** button on the toolbar. The Comments pane opens; you can see comments from others and see who has clicked that particular photo's Like button (see Figure 7.26). You can converse about the photo by entering your own comments and clicking **Post**.

To add photos to a shared stream, open the stream and click the **Add Photos** button. Select and add photos in the same way as when you created the shared stream.

FIGURE 7.26 You can view the comments others have made as well as post your own.

To change the stream, open it and click the **Options** button. On the resulting dialog box, you can do the following:

▶ Change the stream's name.

▶ See the status of current subscribers.

▶ Add or remove subscribers.

▶ Resend invitations.

▶ Change the status of the public website option.

To remove a shared stream, right-click on the stream and choose **Delete**. Click **Delete** in the resulting dialog box, and the stream is removed. The photos remain on your computer—only the shared stream is impacted.

Working with Shared Photo Streams in Windows

When a stream is shared with you, you see a notification, and the stream appears in your Photo Stream folder (you don't see thumbnails unless you subscribe to it). You see the name of the stream and who wants to share it with you. Right-click the stream and choose **Accept** to subscribe to it or **Decline** if you don't want to subscribe. If you accept it, you are subscribed to the stream and it becomes active in your Photo Stream.

You can work with streams being shared with you in the following ways:

▶ **Browse and view its photos**—Double-click a shared stream to see the photos it contains.

▶ **Import photos to your photo application**—To add shared photos to your own photo application, open that application and import the photos in the shared stream the same as you would from any other location on your computer. The photos you import are downloaded from the shared stream and become like other photos you have added to that application.

▶ **Comment/Like**—Click the **Comments** button. The Comments area opens. Select the photo you want to comment on. Enter your comments and click **Post** (see Figure 7.27). Click **Like** to indicate that you like the photo.

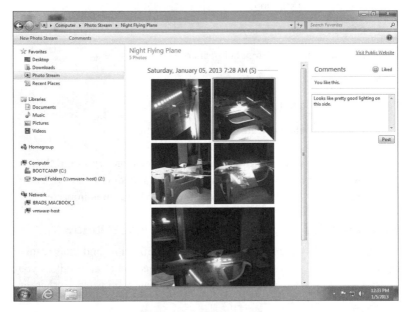

FIGURE 7.27   You can comment on and like photos being shared with you.

▶ **Remove a shared stream**—To get rid of a shared stream, perform a right-click on it and choose **Unsubscribe**. Confirm the action at the prompt, and it is removed from your Photo Stream.

Using Photo Stream with an Apple TV

An Apple TV is a great way to view your photos. Prior to Photo Stream, you had to sync your photos to some other device to be able to view them using an Apple TV. With Photo Stream, you can view photos on your Apple TV automatically.

> NOTE: **Apple TV Requirements**
>
> To use Photo Stream with an Apple TV, it must be running Apple TV software version 5.1 or later.

Enabling Photo Stream on an Apple TV

To enable Photo Stream, perform the following steps:

1. Start up the Apple TV.

2. Select **Photo Stream** on the main menu.

3. If you've already configured your iCloud account on the Apple TV, select **Yes**; if you want to use a different account, select **No, use a different account** and follow the prompts to enter the account you want to use. The Apple TV connects to your iCloud account.

4. If you want your Photo Stream to be your Apple TV's screen saver, select **Yes**; if you want to keep the current screen saver, select **No**. When you move to the Photo Stream screen, your photos start to download. The amount of time it takes to download all of them depends on the number of photos you have and your connection speed. You can start viewing photos as others download.

Viewing Your Photo Stream on an Apple TV

To view your Photo Stream, select **Photo Stream** on the main menu if you aren't already on the Photo Stream screen. When you move to the Photo Stream screen, you see thumbnails for all the photos in your Photo Stream. Here, you can do the following:

▶ Open any of the Photo Streams available, which include your Photo Streams along with any that you are sharing or that are being shared with you.

▶ When you open a Photo Stream, you see thumbnails of the images it contains. Use the remote to browse these. To see a photo at full size, select its **thumbnail** and press the Select button on the remote; you move to the next or previous photo using the remote. Press **menu** on the remote to move back to the Photo Stream's screen.

▶ To view the photos in Photo Stream in a slideshow, open the Photo Stream and select the **Slideshow** button. On the resulting screen, you can configure how photos in the slideshow are presented (such as shuffle or repeat), choose the music (the playlist) you want to hear while the slideshow plays, and select the slideshow's theme. When you are done configuring options, select the **Start Slideshow** button.

▶ To use the photos in a Photo Stream as your screen saver, open the Photo Stream, select the **Screen Saver** button, and select **Yes**.

▶ When a photo has comments, it is marked with the quote bubble icon. To view the comments and "like" status of a photo, view it and press the **Select** button on the remote. Thumbnails appear for each photo, and you can see the comments and like status of the current one. Use the remote to move to other photos in the shared Photo Stream.

► To indicate you like a shared photo, view and press the **Select** button on the remote. Then press the **Select** button again and the photo's status will reflect that you like it.

► To remove a shared Photo Stream, open it and select the **Unsubscribe** button.

Summary

In this lesson, you learned how to use Photo Stream to make your photos available on your iOS devices, Macintoshes, Windows PCs, and Apple TVs. In the next lesson, you learn how to use iCloud with your documents.

LESSON 8

Using iCloud with Your Documents

In this lesson, you learn how to use iCloud to work with the same documents on iOS devices, Macs, and Windows PCs. You also learn about the iWork area of your iCloud website.

Syncing Documents with iCloud

Creating, editing, and producing documents, such as text, spreadsheets, and presentations, are some of the primary reasons computers and related devices are so incredibly useful. However, when you work on the same documents on different devices, it can be cumbersome to make sure you are working with the most recent version of your documents on each device. There are lots of ways to share your documents on your devices, including storing documents in folders that get synced on your devices, emailing versions of documents to yourself on a device, and storing documents on the cloud so that you can access them on all your devices. As you can probably guess from the title of this lesson, iCloud can help you with the task of syncing your documents. Because they can be stored on the cloud, you can access the same documents from different devices.

Document syncing via iCloud is a mixed bag because, unlike the other iCloud services, it works quite differently based on the specific device and apps you are using.

You may find yourself in a number of different situations that determine how useful iCloud document syncing is to you. These include the following:

▶ **iCloud-aware apps that store documents on the cloud**—If you use one of the iCloud-aware apps (the primary ones being Pages, Keynote, and Numbers), you can access the same documents on Macs and iOS devices (as long as the related apps are installed on each device). Some iCloud-aware apps, such as TextEdit and Preview, are only available on Macs, so you can use iCloud to share their documents on only those types of computers. Unfortunately, at press time, there are no iCloud-aware apps for Windows PCs, so if you primarily use Windows, this option is not available to you.

▶ **iCloud-aware apps that sync documents on the cloud**—Some iCloud-aware apps have a built-in sync function that ensures the same versions of documents are available on each device. If the app you use has both a Mac and iOS version, you can use the app to keep documents in sync on these devices. Unfortunately, there are currently no iCloud-aware apps like this for Windows PCs.

NOTE: **Windows Syncing**

Currently, the only iCloud-aware apps available are for Macs and iOS devices and are only available in the Mac and iOS App Stores, thus greatly reducing the value of iCloud document syncing for Windows users. If you use primarily Windows PCs for working on documents or you don't use iCloud-aware apps on any platform, there are better document-syncing options for you (see the following sidebar for one example).

▶ **Apps that aren't iCloud aware but that use documents in one of the supported formats**—Some documents are supported in iCloud even if you don't use an iCloud-aware app to work with them. Primary examples are Word, PowerPoint, Excel, and the Comma Separated Values (CSV) format. For these types, you can use iCloud to manually store the documents on the cloud, where you can download them onto computers so that you can work with them.

▶ **Apps that aren't iCloud aware and don't use documents that
are in one of the supported formats**—If you are using a document that isn't in one of the supported formats, iCloud won't
help you keep it in sync, so you need to use a different solution.

PLAIN ENGLISH: **Dropbox**

If you primarily use Windows PCs for working on documents or if you
use a Mac but not the iCloud-aware apps, I recommend you use
Dropbox instead of iCloud for document syncing. Dropbox is available for free (www.dropbox.com) for all platforms (Windows, Macs,
and iOS, as well as other mobile operating systems such as Android
for that matter). Dropbox enables you to easily store any type of document on the cloud so you can access it from any device. It also
enables you to easily share documents and folders of documents
with others, which makes it a great collaboration tool. When you
aren't using an iCloud-aware app, Dropbox is much more convenient
because you can access it directly from the desktop on Macs and
Windows PCs instead of having to use a web browser.

Because of its limitations, document syncing is probably the least useful
feature that iCloud offers—unless you primarily use iCloud-aware apps—
but it is good to understand how this feature works so that you can decide
if iCloud document syncing will be helpful to you.

The first step is to enable iCloud document syncing on each device. From
there, read the sections that relate to your situation: using iCloud-aware
apps or manually syncing documents.

Enabling iCloud Document Syncing

Like with the other iCloud services, you need to enable iCloud document
syncing on each device where you will use it. See the following sections
for the types of devices you use.

Enabling iCloud Document Syncing on iOS Devices

To enable an iOS device to sync documents, perform the following steps:

1. Open the Settings app.

2. Tap **iCloud**.

3. Tap **Documents & Data**.

4. Set the **Documents & Data** switch to ON, as shown in Figure 8.1. This configures the device to use iCloud to store documents in the cloud so that you can sync them on your devices.

FIGURE 8.1   Set the Documents & Data switch to the ON position to store your documents in the cloud.

5. If you are configuring a device that supports a cellular data network, set the **Use Cellular Data** switch to ON if you want document syncing to occur when you are using the cellular network. Set it to OFF if you only want document syncing to occur when you are using a Wi-Fi network. If your cellular data account has a limit on the amount of data you can transfer, you might want to leave this in the OFF position so that document syncing doesn't use up a significant portion of your monthly data allotment or result in overage charges (which can be very expensive).

TIP: **Temp Syncing**

If you do disable the Use Cellular Data setting and are working on a document while you only have access to your cellular network, you can always go back to the Documents & Data screen and temporarily enable cellular syncing to ensure the document gets copied to the cloud. Then, turn this setting to OFF again so that you don't use up your monthly data allotment to avoid getting hit with overage charges.

Enabling iCloud Document Syncing on Macs

To use iCloud document syncing on a Mac, ensure that your iCloud account is set to sync documents by performing the following steps:

1. Open the System Preferences application.

2. Click the **iCloud** icon. The iCloud pane appears.

3. Ensure the **Documents & Data** check box is checked, as shown in Figure 8.2.

FIGURE 8.2   Check the Documents & Data check box to sync your documents on a Mac.

> NOTE: **No Windows Document Sync**
>
> There is no Documents & Data setting for Windows because true iCloud document syncing is not supported on the Windows platform. You use the manual upload and download process via a web browser.

Syncing Documents Using iCloud-Aware Apps

iCloud document syncing is the most useful when you are using iCloud-aware apps. As with all things iCloud document syncing related, there are further complexities because of the different ways even iCloud-aware apps support this functionality.

> NOTE: **Windows Users Can Skip Ahead**
>
> If you primarily use Windows to work on documents, the information in this section is of no value to you, so skip ahead to "Manually Syncing Documents Through iCloud."

Some iCloud-aware apps, notably Pages, Keynote, and Numbers, are available for both Macs and iOS devices. This enables you to access the same documents on any device of these types (of course, you need to have the related app, such as Pages, to be able to work with a document).

Some iCloud-aware apps, such as Preview, are available only for Macs. In this case, you can access the same documents on all your Macs.

The first two cases are covered in the section "Using Apps That Store Documents on the Cloud."

The third type of situation is those apps that have both Mac and iOS versions available and support an iCloud syncing function that causes the app to ensure that the document is updated to the current version on all devices (one example is Tap Forms, which is a database app). This situation is covered in the section "Using Apps That Sync Documents via the Cloud."

Using Apps That Store Documents on the Cloud

A number of apps can store documents on the cloud so that you can access the same document from multiple devices. Some of these apps have versions for Macs and for iOS devices (such as the often-mentioned Pages, Keynote, and Numbers), whereas others just have versions for Macs (TextEdit and Preview being two examples).

You need to install the apps you want to use on each device. Fortunately, you only have to pay for apps you get from the Mac or iOS App Stores once and you can download and install them on multiple devices. (You do have to pay for the Mac and iOS versions of these apps.)

Some of the apps, such as TextEdit and Preview, are available by default in OS X, so you don't need to install those.

Enabling Document Syncing in iCloud-Aware Apps on iOS Devices

In addition to enabling iCloud document syncing at the device level (via the iCloud Settings screen covered earlier), you must also enable or disable this feature for each app you use. There are two ways in which document syncing can be enabled for iOS apps.

The first time you launch an app, you're prompted to store your documents, as shown in Figure 8.3. Tap **Use iCloud** to enable iCloud document syncing.

> NOTE: **iWork Apps Only**
> As mentioned previously, when this book was written, only Apple's iWork apps supported iCloud document syncing. Hopefully, other apps add this support—in which case, it is likely they will work very similarly.

You can enable or disable iCloud document syncing at any time by opening the Settings app and tapping the icon for the app you want to configure; for example, tap **Keynote** to enable or disable document syncing for the Keynote app. On the app's Setting screen, set the **Use iCloud** switch to the ON position to enable document syncing, as shown in Figure 8.4.

Set it to the OFF position if you only want the documents to be stored on the device.

FIGURE 8.3 When you launch an iOS app for the first time, you're prompted to enable iCloud document syncing.

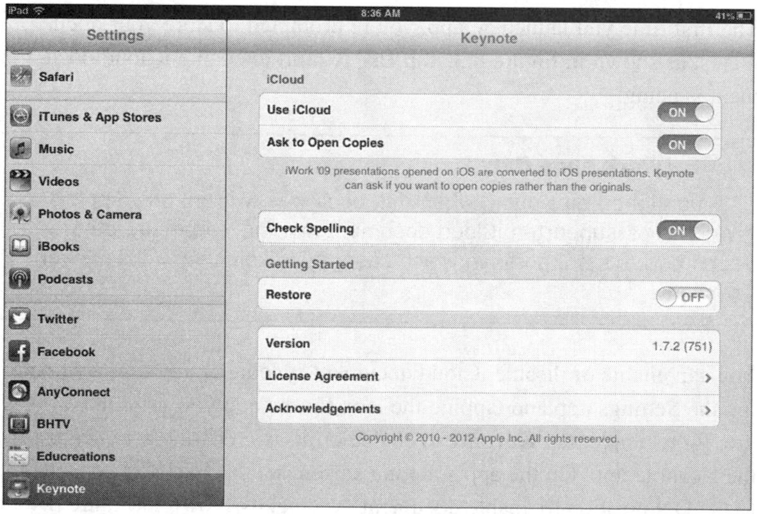

FIGURE 8.4 iCloud document syncing is enabled for the Keynote app.

When iCloud document syncing is enabled, any documents with which you are working and any documents you create are automatically stored on the cloud along with documents created on other devices that also have iCloud document syncing enabled for the same apps.

Working with Documents in iCloud-Aware Apps on iOS Devices

Any iOS apps' documents that are stored on the cloud are automatically available in those apps for which iCloud document syncing is enabled. When you open the document management area of the app, you see all its documents that are on the cloud, as shown in Figure 8.5.

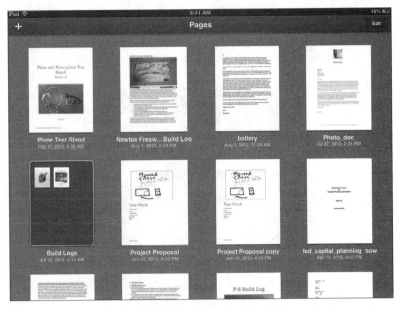

FIGURE 8.5   Documents stored on the cloud are shown on the document management screen in iOS apps (Pages, in this case).

To work with a document, tap it. It opens in the app, and you can work with it as you normally would.

> **NOTE: Edited on Mac**
> Although documents in the same app on a Mac or iOS device are almost exactly the same, there are can be some minor differences. When you open a document that has been edited on a Mac, you see a prompt informing you of this. Then, you see a window showing you the specific differences. Review this information and tap **Open** to work on the document.

Following are some other aspects of iCloud syncing that will help you work with it:

▶ When a document needs to be updated (on the cloud), its icon has a folded corner, as shown in Figure 8.6. Modified documents are uploaded automatically, so you don't need to take action; this lets you know that you should let the upload process happen before working with the document on other devices.

FIGURE 8.6   This document has been modified and needs to be uploaded to the cloud.

▶ As documents are uploaded, you see progress bars in the documents' icons and a status message in the upper-right corner of the screen (which shows how many documents are being updated).

When the progress bar disappears, the updated documents are available on the cloud and on other synced devices.

▶ It's possible for the versions of a document to get out of sync if it is being edited on two different devices at the same time. This can also happen if you work on a document using a device that isn't connected to the Internet and then work on the same document on a second device. When you reconnect the first device, iCloud won't know which version it should use as the master. Whenever there is a conflict between versions of a document, you are presented with a dialog box that enables you to choose the version you want to use as the master for that document. Tap the version you want to keep and then tap **Keep**. The version you selected becomes the master version stored on the cloud and subsequently is available on other synced devices.

iCloud document syncing works very well with the iOS apps that support it; in fact, most of the time, it will be transparent to you, which is exactly how you want syncing to work. You don't even have to think about it because the iCloud service manages the process for you.

Working with Documents in iCloud-Aware Apps on Macs

A number of apps available for Macs are iCloud aware. On a Mac, this means you have the option to directly save documents to and open documents from the cloud.

To save a document on the cloud, making it available to other devices using iCloud-enabled apps, open the Save sheet and choose **iCloud** on the **Where** menu (see Figure 8.7). The document is saved on the cloud and can be opened from other Macs or iOS devices using the same iCloud-aware app.

To open a document that is stored on the cloud, use the Open command and on the resulting dialog box click the **iCloud** button. You see the documents that are stored on the cloud. Select the document you want and click **Open** (see Figure 8.8). The document is opened within the app and you can work with it as you would any other sort of document. When you save the document, the edited version is saved on the cloud and is available to other synced devices.

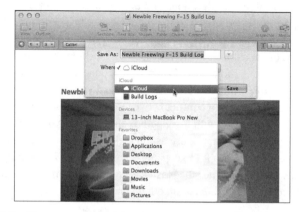

FIGURE 8.7   When you select iCloud on the Where menu, a document is saved on the cloud.

FIGURE 8.8   When you choose iCloud in the Open dialog for an iCloud-enabled app, you can open documents stored on the cloud.

TIP: **Work Locally**

When you use an iCloud-aware app on a Mac, you still have the option to store the document on the Mac's drive. You can choose any location on your Mac by using the **Where** menu.

Using Apps That Sync Documents via the Cloud

Some apps support iCloud syncing directly within the app. You usually enable this function and then manually start the sync process. The app then checks each version of the document on each device and ensures that all have the same version available, so that you know the current one is on each device.

Of course, you need to have the app installed on each Mac and iOS device on which you want to use the document.

To get started, enable iCloud syncing. On a Mac app, this is usually done through the preferences settings for that app. In Figure 8.9, you see iCloud Sync being enabled in the database app Tap Forms. On an iOS device, this is typically done through the settings within the device, such as the iCloud settings.

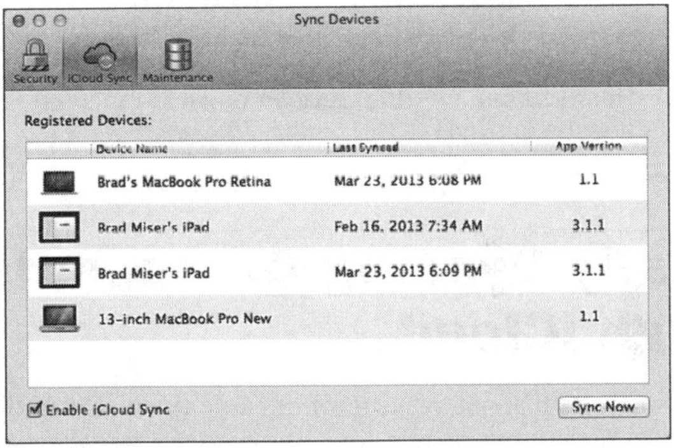

FIGURE 8.9 Enable the iCloud syncing function in an app to synchronize documents across multiple devices.

To sync documents, you activate the sync function within the app; Figure 8.10 shows this being done in the Tap Forms app on an iOS device. Typically, you tap the **Sync** button in the app. When the app syncs, it uploads any changed information from the current device to the cloud and downloads updated information from the other devices with which it is synced, thus ensuring each device has the same version of the document or information.

FIGURE 8.10   Here you can see the devices on which the Tap Forms app is keeping its databases in sync.

Manually Syncing Documents Through iCloud

iCloud also supports manual syncing of documents, meaning that you store documents in the iWork area of your iCloud website. You can download those documents onto a device, work on them, and then upload the updated version back to the site. You can do the same process on other devices so that you can share a single version of a document among all of them.

For this process, you are limited to files of the following types:

- ▶ Pages
- ▶ Keynote
- ▶ Numbers

▶ PowerPoint

▶ Word

▶ Excel

▶ TXT (text)

▶ CSV (Comma Separated Values)

You need to have the corresponding or compatible apps installed on a device to be able to work with the documents you download. For example, to use a Pages document in Word on a Windows PC, you can save it as a Word document and then open it within Word. If you have the same app on different devices, such as Pages on a Mac and an iOS device, the documents should open relatively seamlessly on each device (there may be minor differences).

TIP: **Saving in Other Formats**

To save some types of documents in a different format, such as a Pages document as a Word document, you need to save them to the computer's drive first and then upload the new versions to your iWork website.

You can open documents from Windows apps, such as Word, directly in Word on a Mac or the corresponding iWork app, such as Pages for Word docs.

You may have to do some experimentation to see which types of files work best on the specific platforms you use.

As you can see, this option has more caveats that other iCloud services. How useful it will be to you depends on the specific combination of platforms and apps you use.

Using Your iWork Website

As you learned in Lesson 1, "Getting Started with Your iCloud Account and Website," your iCloud account includes a website that has applications you can use. One of these is the iWork area, which is where you access documents directly on the cloud. To use iCloud document syncing with Macs or Windows PCs, you need to download or upload documents you want to sync via your website.

To access your documents, perform the following steps (if you need help accessing your iCloud website, refer to Lesson 1):

1. Log in to your iCloud website.

2. Open the iWork app on the website.

3. Click the application tab for the documents with which you want to work, such as **Keynote**, **Pages**, or **Numbers**. You see the documents from the application, or a related one, that are stored in the cloud, as shown in Figure 8.11. For example, documents stored in the Word format also appear on the Pages tab.

FIGURE 8.11   You can use your iCloud website to access your documents on the cloud.

4. Select the document with which you want to work and select a command on the menu that appears when you click the **Action** (gear) button or just click the **Action** button and use the **Upload** command to upload a document.

TIP: **Creating Folders on Your iWork Website**

To create a folder on your iWork website, open the related document on an iOS device. For example, to add a folder to your Pages tab, open Pages on an iPad, iPhone, or iPod touch. On the document selection screen, drag one document on top of another one. A folder containing those two documents is created, and you are prompted to give the folder a name. Do so and tap **Done**. Drag more documents onto the folder to add them to it and tap **Done** when you are finished.

When a document is selected, open the Action menu to perform any of the following actions:

▶ Choose **Download Document** to download the document to a computer. What happens after you download the document depends on the format you selected and the type of computer you use to download it (the options are explained in the following sections).

▶ Choose **Delete Document** to remove the document from your website.

CAUTION: **Deleting Documents**

When you delete a document from your website, it is also deleted from any iOS devices. If you want to keep a version of the document, download it to a computer before you delete it.

▶ Choose **Duplicate Document** to create a copy of the document. Copies you create become available on synced iOS devices too.

TIP: **Opening Folders on Your iWork Website**

To open a folder in your iWork website, click it. The folder opens and you see the documents it contains so that you can open them.

▶ Choose **Sort by Name** to sort the documents by name or choose **Sort by Date** to sort them by date.

TIP: **Other Ways to Download and Upload**

You can download a document by pointing to it and clicking the **Download** button that appears. You can upload a document by dragging it from your desktop and dropping it onto the related tab of your iWork website.

You can also upload documents to the cloud from a Mac or Windows PC to make them available to other devices. Click the tab corresponding to the type of document you want to upload, click the **Action** button, and choose **Upload** *documenttype*, where *documenttype* is the type of document you are uploading, such as Presentation when you are on the Keynote tab. Move to and select the document you want to upload. Press the **Return** key (Mac) or **Enter** key (Windows). The document is uploaded to your website. While the document is being uploaded, you see a message like the one in Figure 8.12, to monitor the process. When the process finishes, you see the document on your website.

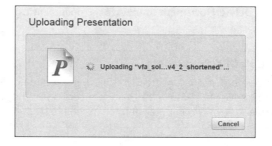

FIGURE 8.12 Upload your documents to the cloud to make them available on other devices.

NOTE: **Manually Uploaded Docs in iCloud-Aware Apps**

When you manually upload a document from your iWork website, it immediately becomes available in iCloud-aware apps on Macs and iOS devices. For example, if you upload a Word document to your iWork website on a Windows PC, that document immediately becomes available in Pages on an iOS device.

Manually Syncing Documents Stored in the Cloud on Macs

In the previous section, " Using Your iWork Website," you pretty much learned everything you need to know to use iCloud to manually sync documents on your Mac.

When you are ready to work on a document, download it from your website as follows:

1. Move to the iWork area of your iCloud website.

TIP: **More Convenient Document Syncing**

When you log in to iCloud, make sure you check the check box so you remain signed in. To make syncing documents more convenient, open a separate web browser window or tab and move to your iWork website. Leave the iWork window or open at all times (you can minimize a separate window to the Dock to move it out of your way or use Mission Control to add it to a desktop space). Or, you can add a bookmark to your site so you can quickly move back to it. Using these methods, you can quickly jump into the iWork window to download or upload documents.

---

2. Click the tab for the type of document you want to work with, such as **Keynote, Pages**, or **Numbers**.

3. Click the document you want to use.

4. Click **Download**.

5. Click the file format you want; the options depend on the type of document you are working with. For example, if you selected Pages in step 2, the options may be Pages, PDF, and Word, as shown in Figure 8.13. These options that are active depend on the specific file you clicked in step 3; for example, if it is a Word document, only the Word option is available. iCloud prepares the file and then downloads it. After the file downloads, it opens in the application associated with the file type you downloaded (for example, if you selected the Pages format, the file opens in the Pages app).

FIGURE 8.13 When you download a Pages document, you can choose Pages, PDF, or Word, depending on the application you want to use with the document.

6. Use the application to work with the document.

NOTE: **Where'd It Go?**

When you download a document from iCloud, it is stored in your designated download folder, which is the Downloads folder in your Home folder by default. To see the current download folder, open your browser's preferences and see where it downloads files. (In Safari, this is on the General tab of the Preferences dialog box.)

When you finish working with a document, you need to upload it to your iCloud website so it is synced to your iOS devices and becomes available to download onto other computers.

To upload the document, perform the following steps:

1. Move your iCloud web window so that it is visible on the desktop.

2. Click the tab for the type of document you are uploading, such as **Keynote**, **Pages**, or **Numbers**.

3. Drag the file from your desktop onto the web window, as shown in Figure 8.14.

FIGURE 8.14   To upload a document on which you've worked, drag it from the desktop onto the iWork page.

4. If you've previously downloaded the document and want to replace the version on the website with the version you modified, click **Replace**. The updated file is stored in your iWork area, where it is copied onto synced devices (the next time you open the associated app), and is available to be downloaded to other computers. (If you want to store a different version on the website instead, click **Cancel**, rename the file, and upload it again.)

Manually Syncing Documents Stored in the Cloud on Windows PCs

In the earlier section, "Using Your iWork Website," you pretty much learned everything you need to know to use iCloud to sync documents on your Windows PC.

To sync your documents, you need to perform two steps. When you are ready to work on a document, download it to your computer. When you've finished working on it, upload it to your iCloud website so it is available to other devices.

To download a document, perform the following steps:

1. Move to the iWork area of your iCloud website.

> TIP: **More Convenient Document Syncing**
> When you log in to iCloud, make sure you check the check box so you remain signed in. To make syncing documents more convenient, open a separate web browser window or tab and move to your iWork area. Leave the iWork window or open at all times (you can minimize a separate window to move it out of your way). Or, set a bookmark for your website so you can quickly return to it at any time. With these techniques, you can quickly jump into the iWork window to download or upload documents.

2. Click the tab for the type of document you want to work with, such as **Keynote**, **Pages**, or **Numbers**.

3. Click the **document** you want to use.

4. Click **Download**.

5. Click the file format you want; the options depend on the type of document you are working with. For example, if you selected Keynote in step 2, the options are **Keynote**, **PDF**, and **PowerPoint** (see Figure 8.15). iCloud prepares the file for download.

6. Respond to any prompts you see, such as when you want to open or save the document.

7. To save your document to your computer, click **Save**. The document is saved to your default downloads location.

8. Use the related application to work with the document.

When you're done working with a document, you need to upload it to your iCloud website so it will be synced to your iOS devices and available to download onto other computers.

FIGURE 8.15 Here, I'm downloading a presentation in the PowerPoint format so I can use that application to work on it.

To upload the document, perform the following steps:

1. Move your iCloud web window so that it is visible on the desktop.

2. Click the tab for the type of document you are uploading, such as **Keynote**, **Pages**, or **Numbers**.

3. Drag the file from your desktop onto the web window.

4. If you've previously downloaded the document and want to replace the version on the website with the version you modified, click **Replace**. The updated file is stored in your iWork area from where it is copied onto synced iOS devices (the next time you open the associated app) and is available to be downloaded to other computers. (If you want to store a different version on the website instead, click **Cancel**, rename the file, and upload it again.)

NOTE: **Can't Upload?**

If you receive an error message when you try to upload a document, the file type you are trying to upload probably isn't supported or you might not have the correct tab selected (such as Keynote for presentations).

Summary

In this lesson, you learned how to use your iCloud account to sync documents on your devices. In the next lesson, you learn how to use iCloud for email.

Configuring Your iCloud Email

In this lesson, you learn how to configure your devices to work with your iCloud email and to use the iCloud email web application.

Working with iCloud Email

An iCloud account includes email service, which you can access via iOS devices, Macintosh computers, and Windows PCs. You can also work with your iCloud email using the email application available on your iCloud website; this enables you to use your iCloud email on any device that has a compatible web browser and Internet connection.

If you choose to use it, your iCloud email address is the Apple ID associated with your iCloud account. In most cases, this is something like *youraccountname*@icloud.com, where *youraccountname* is the name you chose when you created your Apple ID account. You can also use a different email address as your Apple ID, such as a Google email address; if you choose this route, you create an iCloud email address when you create your iCloud account.

This lesson explains how to configure iCloud email on each type of device. iCloud email is designed to work in the Mail app on iOS devices, in Mail on Macintosh computers, and in Outlook on Windows PCs. You can also set up other applications to work with your iCloud email account in the event you don't want to use one of the default email applications.

> NOTE: **Back in Time**
> iCloud is the third major iteration of Apple's online service. Each has had its unique domain. The very first was way back when the service was for Mac users only and the domain was .mac. Next came MobileMe with its domain being .me. Now we have iCloud. Email addresses under the previous iterations are still valid, so you may see the .mac or .me domains from time to time. You may have noticed that my Apple ID has the .mac domain—I've been using this service for a long time!

Setting Up iCloud Email on iOS Devices

Assuming you've already configured your iCloud account on an iOS device as explained in Lesson 2, "Configuring iCloud on an iPhone, iPod touch, or iPad," you need to ensure that Mail is enabled for your iCloud account. You can also configure other options for your iCloud email.

Enabling iCloud Email on an iOS Device

Open the Settings app, tap **iCloud**, and ensure the **Mail** switch is set to the ON position, as shown in Figure 9.1. This configures the Mail app to use your iCloud email account.

FIGURE 9.1   Set the Mail switch to the ON position to activate your iCloud email account in the Mail app.

That's all you have to do to start using your iCloud email account in the Mail app. When you open the Mail app, you see your iCloud account listed on the Mailboxes screen, as shown in Figure 9.2. You can tap the **iCloud inbox** to view your iCloud messages or tap **All Inboxes** to see the messages in all your accounts. To work with your iCloud email account folders, tap **iCloud** in the Accounts section. (Of course, if you changed your iCloud account's description, the description you created appears instead of "iCloud.")

NOTE: **One and Only Account?**

If your iCloud email account is the only one enabled on your device, you see the folders for your iCloud email account on the Mailboxes screen. You tap any of the listed folders to access them. For example, to see your messages, tap **Inbox**.

FIGURE 9.2   When you enable your iCloud email account, it appears in the Mail app.

Determining How iCloud Email Is Synced on an iOS Device

As you learned in Lesson 2, you can configure how and how often iCloud information is updated on your iOS device. For iCloud email, you have three options: Push, Fetch, and Manual (see Lesson 2 for an explanation of these options). To determine how your iCloud email information is synced, follow these steps:

1. Open the Settings app.

2. Tap **Mail, Contacts, Calendars**.

3. Tap **Fetch New Data**.

4. Tap **Advanced**.

5. Tap your iCloud account.

6. Tap **Push**, **Fetch**, or **Manual**. Your iCloud email is synced on the device according to the setting you select. If you select Manual, open the Mail app to sync your email.

NOTE: **Don't Push Me!**

Even if you disable Push on the Fetch New Data screen, the Push option is available for your iCloud email. However, if you select it, email is synced using Fetch as long as Push is disabled on your device. So, you need to ensure that the Push switch is in the ON position on the Fetch New Data screen if you want your iCloud email to be pushed to your device.

Changing Global Email Settings on an iOS Device

To make changes that impact all of your email accounts (not just your iCloud email account), complete the following steps:

1. Move to the Mail, Contacts, Calendars screen.

2. If necessary, scroll down until you see the Mail section.

3. Tap **Show**.

4. Tap the number of recent messages you want to display in the Mail app.

5. Tap the Return button (which is labeled **Mail...** on iPhones and iPod touches and labeled **Mail, Contacts...** on an iPad).

6. Tap **Preview**.

7. Tap the number of lines you want to display for each email message when you view the inbox. This enables you to read part of the message without opening it.

8. Tap the **Return** button.

9. Set the **Show To/Cc Label** slider to ON to always see the To and Cc labels in email headers. (With this disabled, you can view this information on a message by tapping Details.)

10. If you don't want to confirm your action when you delete messages, set the **Ask Before Deleting** switch to OFF. When you delete a message, it immediately goes into the trash.

11. If you want images in HTML email messages to be displayed automatically when you read messages, set the **Load Remote Images** switch to ON. If you disable this feature by setting it to OFF, you can manually load images in a message. If you receive a lot of spam, you should disable this so that you won't see images in which you might not be interested and to avoid any chance that images can be used to validate your email address.

12. If you don't want Mail to organize your messages by thread (which means grouping them based on their subjects so that you see all the messages on a single topic on the same screen), disable this feature by setting the **Organize by Thread** switch to OFF. With this setting disabled, messages are listed individually in your Inbox. With this setting enabled, messages on the same topic are grouped together.

13. If you don't want to receive a blind copy of each email you send, set **Always Bcc Myself** to OFF. If you set the status to

ON, each time you send a message, you also receive a copy of it, but your address is not shown to the message's other recipients.

14. Tap **Increase Quote Level**.

15. If you don't want Mail to automatically indent current content (quoted content) when you reply or forward email, set the **Increase Quote Level** switch to OFF. Generally, you should leave this enabled (ON) so it is easier for the recipients to tell when you have added content versus that quoted content.

16. Tap the **Return** button.

17. Tap **Signature**. This enables you to create a signature block that is automatically added to messages you send. You can use the same signature for messages from all your accounts or you can use a different signature for each account.

18. To use the same signature for all your accounts, tap **All Accounts**. To use a different signature for each account, tap **Per Account**. (If you only have one email account configured on your device, you don't have these options.)

19. If you tapped All Accounts, tap in the signature block. If you tapped Per Account, tap in the signature block for the first account for which you want to create a signature—by default, the signature is "Sent from my *device*" where *device* is the name of the device you are configuring. The keyboard appears.

20. Enter the signature you want to append to each message you send from all your accounts or from the account for which you chose to enter a signature. If you don't want an automatic signature, delete all the text on the screen. You can include links or graphics in your signature by either typing them in or pasting them, as shown in Figure 9.3.

21. If you selected the Per Account option, tap in the signature block for the next account.

22. Repeat steps 20 and 21 until you have created a signature for each of your accounts.

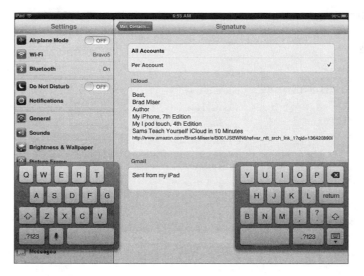

FIGURE 9.3   You can configure a signature that is automatically added to your email messages.

23. Tap the **Return** button. You see the number of signatures you have configured in the Signatures block, or you see a preview of the signature you have created if you are using only one.

24. Tap **Default Account**. If you have only one email account configured on the device, this option doesn't apply and you can skip the rest of these steps.

25. Tap the account you want to be your default. The default account appears at the top of lists and is automatically selected as the From address for emails you create as new messages. (Of course, you can change the From address on messages when you create them.) It is also the one used when you send photos, YouTube videos, and so on.

26. Tap the **Return** button. You have now completed configuring the functional aspects of the Mail app, as shown in Figure 9.4.

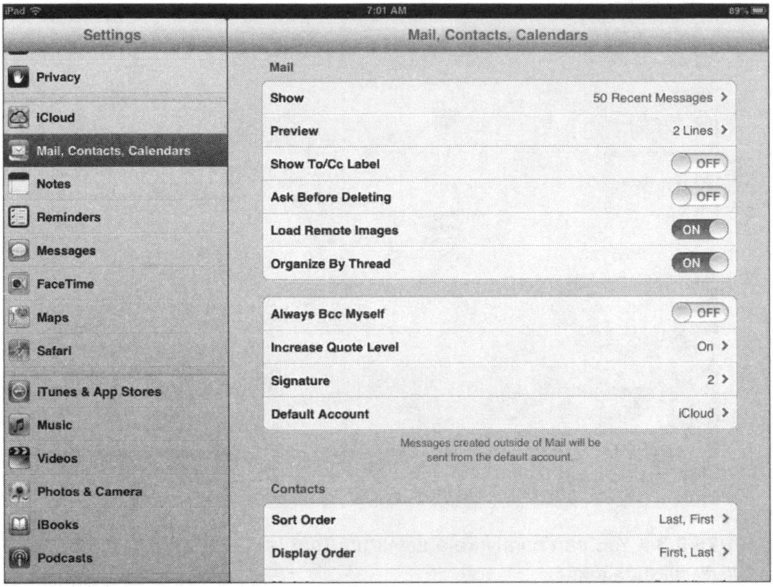

FIGURE 9.4   Use the Mail, Contacts, Calendars screen to configure email options.

TIP: **Changing Text Size**

If you want to change the size of the text used in Mail along with other apps on your device, open the Settings app and tap **General**, tap **Accessibility**, and the tap **Large Text**. Tap the size of text you want to be used in Mail, Contacts, Calendars, and other apps; the options range from 20 pt to 56 pt. To use the default size, tap **Off**.

You how you are notified when mail actions happen. Notifications can be both audible and visible, or you can choose to use just one type. You can also set different notifications options for each email account you use.

To set the default audible notifications (which are used unless you change them for specific accounts), do the following:

1. Move into the Settings app if you aren't there already.

2. Tap **Sounds**.

3. Tap **New Mail**.

4. Tap the sound you want to play when you receive new mail or tap **None** if you don't want a sound to play. When you tap a sound, you hear it, and it is marked with a check mark showing you it is the selected sound.

TIP: **Good Vibrations**

If you are using an iPhone or iPod touch, you can also configure vibrations for new mail and sent mail. On the related sound screen, such as New Mail, tap **Vibration** (which appears at the top of the screen) and then tap the vibration pattern you want to use. You can create a custom vibration by tapping **Create New Vibration**, tapping the pattern you want to create, tapping **Stop**, and then tapping **Save**. You can name the new vibration and then select it by tapping it.

---

5. Tap **Sounds**.

6. Tap **Sent Mail**.

7. Tap the sound you want to play when you send mail or tap **None** if you don't want a sound to play.

To set the visible email notifications and to customize the audible notifications for specific email accounts, do the following:

1. Move into the Settings app if you aren't there already.

2. Tap **Notifications**.

3. Tap **Mail**. If you have more than one email account configured on the device, you see the Show option at the top of the screen and a section for each email account underneath it. Below those, you see the VIP notifications. If you have only one email account configured, you see the options for that account. (The rest of these steps assume you have more than one account configured on your device.)

4. Tap **Show**.

5. Tap the number of unread messages that you want to be displayed in the Notification Center.

6. Tap the **Return** button (**Mail** on iPhones/iPod touches or **Mail, Contacts, Calendars** on iPads).

7. Tap the first email account for which you want to configure notifications.

8. To include email information on the Notification Center (which opens when you swipe down from the top of the screen), set **Notification Center** to ON. If you don't want this, leave it set to OFF.

9. Tap the **Alert Style** for new email messages. The options are as follows:

   ▶ **None**—No notifications are displayed when you receive a new message.

   ▶ **Banners**—Banners appear at the top of the screen. You see the sender and subject for the new message. You can tap the message to open it in Mail, or you can do nothing and the banner rotates off the screen in a few seconds.

   ▶ **Alerts**—Alerts appear in the center of the screen. You see the message's sender and subject. You can tap the **Dismiss** button to remove the alert or the **Read** button to read the message. You must do one or the other to remove the alert from the screen.

10. To include the number of new messages for the account in the counter on the Mail icon showing how many new email messages you have received, set the **Badge App Icon** slider to the ON position. If you set this to OFF, the account's new messages aren't reflected in the number of new messages displayed in the badge on the Mail icon.

11. To configure a specific sound for new email sent to this account, tap **New Mail Sound**.

12. Set the sound and vibration (iPhone or iPod touch) for new messages received for this account. This works just like setting default sounds (and vibration) described in the previous steps.

13. To include a preview of the message on the Notification Center or Lock screen, set the **Show Preview** switch to ON.

14. To see new email message notifications when your device is locked, set **View in Lock Screen** to ON. When you receive new messages and your device is locked, you see a notification on the Locked screen. If the device is asleep, it wakes up and shows you the notification. If you take no action, the device goes back to sleep.

15. Review the settings for the account (see Figure 9.5). If you are done with them, tap the **Return** button.

FIGURE 9.5   Use this screen to configure how you want to be notified of email activity.

16. Tap the next account for which you want to configure notifications.

17. Repeat steps 8 through 15 to configure the notifications for the account.

18. Repeat steps 16 and 17 for each email account and for your VIPs.

NOTE: **VIP**

The iOS software enables you to designate people as VIPs. Messages from these people appear in a separate mailbox in the Mail app and you can configure specific notifications for these messages. To designate someone as a VIP, open an email message from that person and tap their name in the **From** section. On the resulting screen, tap **Add to VIP**.

Changing iCloud-Specific Email Settings on an iOS Device

To do advanced configuration for only your iCloud account, perform the following steps:

1. Move into the Settings app if you aren't there already.

2. Tap **Mail, Contacts, Calendars**.

3. Tap your iCloud account.

4. Tap **Account**. You see the Account window that you use to change general aspects of your account, such as the storage plan you are using. These options are explained in Lesson 2.

5. Tap **Mail**. You see the Mail window. Here, you can configure your name, the accounts from which you can send email, SMTP servers (where email is sent from), and whether messages you delete are stored in the Archive folder. These options are also explained in Lesson 2.

6. Tap **Advanced**. You see the Advanced window.

7. Tap **Drafts Mailbox**. The Drafts Mailbox window has two sections. One is labeled On My *Device*, where *Device* is the name of the device you are using, and the other is labeled On the Server. The first section has only the Drafts option, whereas the second lists various folders on the iCloud server.

8. To store your draft messages only on your device, tap **Drafts** in the upper section; to store your draft messages on the server, tap one of the folders in the lower section. It's usually better to store drafts on a server folder because you can then get to them from any device. If you store them on your device, they are only available there.

9. Tap **Advanced**.

10. Tap **Sent Mailbox** and then tap a location to determine where your sent messages are stored. This works just like the setting that determines where your draft messages are stored.

11. Tap **Advanced**.

12. Tap **Deleted Mailbox** to set the location for deleted messages. Typically, you are better off storing deleted messages on the device so messages you delete don't use your iCloud storage space.

13. Tap **Advanced**.

14. Tap **Remove**.

15. Tap the amount of time you want to pass before messages you delete are removed from the Trash. It's generally a good idea to set this time relatively short, such as one day or one week so accumulated deleted messages don't use much of your iCloud storage space or device storage space (depending on the selection you made in step 10). (The S/MIME section, which you aren't likely to use, is explained in Lesson 2.)

You're done with the Advanced settings for your iCloud email account and are now ready to use the Mail app to work with your iCloud email.

NOTE: **More Info on the Mail App**

To learn how to use the Mail app, see my book *My iPhone* or *My iPod touch*.

Configuring iCloud Email on a Mac

Mail is OS X's default email application. It is designed to seamlessly work with your iCloud email account. If you've already signed in to your iCloud account on your Mac, you're ready to configure your iCloud email account in Mail. If not, go back to Lesson 3, "Configuring iCloud on Macintosh Computers," to complete that and then come back here.

First, ensure that your iCloud account is set to sync email by performing the following steps:

1. Open the System Preferences application.

2. Click the **iCloud** icon. The iCloud pane appears.

3. Ensure the **Mail** check box is checked, as shown in Figure 9.6. This ensures your iCloud email is synced on your Mac.

FIGURE 9.6   Check the Mail check box on the iCloud pane of the System Preferences app to sync your iCloud email on a Mac.

After you configure an iCloud account on a Mac, the next time you open the Mail application, the email account is configured for you automatically and is ready for you to use or to further configure, as explained in the following steps:

1. Open the Mail application.

2. Choose **Mail**, **Preferences**.

3. Click the **Accounts** tab.

4. Select your iCloud account on the Accounts list in the left pane of the window. The account configuration tools appear in the right pane of the window.

5. Click the **Account Information** tab if it isn't selected already.

6. To temporarily disable the account, uncheck the **Enable this account** check box. This removes the iCloud mailboxes from Mail and stops checking for new messages. Check the check box to reenable the iCloud email account.

NOTE: **Working with Aliases**

iCloud email supports aliases, which are alternate email addresses you can use. The Alias menu on the Account Information tab allows you to work with your aliases. This topic is covered in detail later in this lesson in the section called "Working with Email Aliases."

---

7. To change the description and "From" name for your account, edit the text in the **Description** and **Full Name** fields, respectively. The remaining fields are technical settings that enable you to receive and send email. You should not have to change any of these because they were configured for you automatically.

8. Click the **Mailbox Behaviors** tab.

9. Check the **Store draft message on the server** check box if you want any message drafts to be available on other devices.

10. Check the **Store sent messages on the server** check box to make your sent messages available to all your devices; leave this unchecked if you want messages you send to be stored on the Mac instead.

11. Use the **Sent** pop-up menu to determine when your sent messages are automatically deleted. The options include Never; when they are one week, one day, or one month old; and when you quit Mail.

12. Use the **Junk** check box and pop-up menu to determine how Mail deals with mail classified as junk; these work similarly to the Sent message tools.

13. Use the **Trash** tools to configure how Mail deals with messages you delete. As shown in Figure 9.7, an additional check box determines whether messages you delete are moved into the Trash folder.

FIGURE 9.7 Use the Mailbox Behaviors tab to determine where Mail stores various kinds of emails and whether notes are shown in your Inbox.

14. Click the **Advanced** tab.

15. If you want Mail to check for iCloud email when it checks for message automatically, check the **Include when automatically checking for new messages** check box.

16. If you want to be able to read messages and their attachments when you aren't connected to the Internet, choose **All messages**

and their attachments on the Keep copies of messages for offline viewing pop-up menu. Other options include don't keep copies of any messages, all messages but omit attachments, and only messages I've read. (There are several other settings on the Advanced tab, but you aren't likely to ever need to change them.)

17. Close the Accounts window and save your changes.

You can work with your iCloud email using all of Mail's great tools; this is a good thing because Mail offers lots of great features and functions. And because you can sync your iCloud email with your other devices, the same email messages are available to you no matter which device you happen to be using.

TIP: **Configuring iCloud Email Without Signing In to iCloud**

If you use a Mac that isn't configured with your iCloud account, you can still use your iCloud email with it. Move to the Accounts pane and click the **Add** (**+**) button at the bottom of the Accounts list. Enter your full name, iCloud email address, and iCloud password. Then click Create. Check or uncheck the check boxes to enable or disable Calendar and Chat syncing. Then click **Create**. The iCloud email account is added to Mail, and you can work with it just like an account created for you.

Configuring iCloud Email on Windows PCs

Outlook is an extremely popular email client for Windows PCs. As you can probably guess, you can configure your iCloud email account in Outlook so you can use that application to work with your email. If Outlook is currently open, quit it before continuing in this section.

First, make sure email syncing is enabled by opening the iCloud control panel and checking the **Mail, Contacts, Calendars, & Tasks with Outlook** check box, as shown in Figure 9.8. Then, click **Apply**. You see the Outlook Setup for iCloud progress window. When the setup is complete, click **Done**. You're ready to use Outlook to access your iCloud email. (If you haven't set up iCloud on the PC yet, go back to Lesson 4, "Configuring iCloud on Windows Computers," and do so; then come back here.)

FIGURE 9.8   Check the Mail, Contacts, Calendars, & Tasks with Outlook check box to sync your iCloud email with Outlook on a Windows PC.

NOTE: **Automatic Configuration**

When you enable iCloud email on your computer, your account may be set up for you automatically. If it is, you will see it the next time you open Outlook. In that case, you will only have to enter your password to work with your iCloud email.

Second, do some additional account configuration in Outlook by performing the following steps (which are for Outlook 2010; the steps for Outlook 2007 are similar):

1. Open the Outlook application.

NOTE: **Sign In**

The first time you open Outlook after setting up iCloud email, you're prompted to enter your iCloud account information. Do so and have Outlook remember it so you don't have to enter it each time you open Outlook.

---

2. Click the **File** tab.

3. Click **Info**.

4. Click **Account Settings** and on the resulting menu, click **Account Settings** again. The Account Settings dialog appears.

5. Double-click your iCloud email account. The Change Account dialog box appears.

6. If needed, change your name in the **Your Name** field.

7. If your user password isn't set to be remembered, check the **Remember password** check box.

8. Click the **More Settings** button.

9. Click the **General** tab.

10. In the top box, enter how you want the iCloud email account to be referenced in Outlook. The default is your email address, but you may want to rename it to something like "iCloud email."

11. Click the **Sent Items** tab.

12. Select the **Do not save copies of sent items** radio button if you don't want sent messages to be saved, select the **Save sent items in the following folder on the server** radio button and click the folder in which they should be saved to save sent messages on the server, or select the **Save sent items in the Sent Items folder on this computer** radio button to save these messages on your computer (see Figure 9.9).

13. Click the **Deleted Items** tab.

14. To store your deleted messages on the server, select the **Move deleted items to the following folder on the server** radio button and select the folder in which they should be stored. To not store them on the server, select the **Mark items for deletion but do not move them automatically** radio button instead.

15. Click **OK**. The More Settings dialog box closes and you move back to the Change Account dialog box.

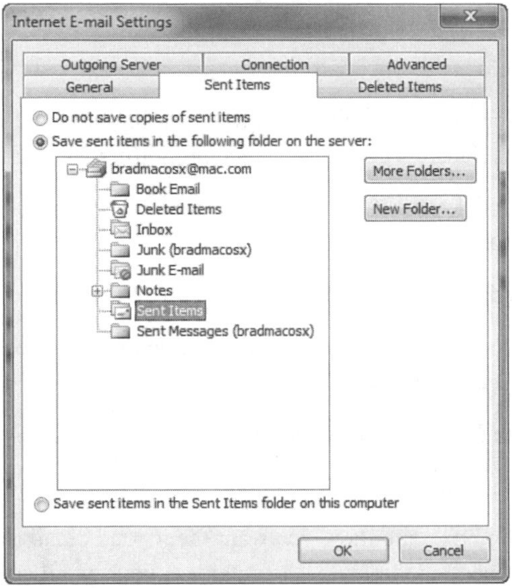

FIGURE 9.9   With this configuration, my sent messages are saved in the Sent Items folder on the server.

16. Click **Next**. Outlook tests your account configuration by sending and receiving email. You receive a test message to your iCloud account.

17. Click **Close**.

18. Click **Finish**.

After you set up your iCloud email account, you can work with it using Outlook's great email tools, just like other accounts with which you use Outlook.

TIP: **Configuring iCloud Email in Other Email Applications**

Although it's designed for Mail on iOS devices and Macs and for Outlook on Windows PCs, you can use your iCloud email account in any email application. You just need to manually configure your iCloud account in those applications. To get the detailed information you need to do this, visit http://support.apple.com/kb/HT4864.

Using the iCloud Mail Web Application

As if the email apps for iOS devices, Macs, and Windows PCs weren't enough ways to use your iCloud email, you can also use the iCloud Mail web application. This application offers several of the same tools you find in a desktop application but has the benefit of being available on any computer running a supported web browser and having an Internet connection.

To access the iCloud email web application, perform the following steps:

1. Log in to your iCloud website (see Lesson 1, "Getting Started with Your iCloud Account and Website," for the details).

2. If you aren't on the Home page (showing the various app icons), click the **Cloud** button in the upper-left corner of the window to move to that page.

3. Click the **Mail** icon. You move into the web email application, as shown in Figure 9.10.

FIGURE 9.10 Using the iCloud Mail web application is a lot like using an email application on a computer.

If you've used an email application before, you won't have any trouble using the Mail web application. The following are some pointers for your consideration:

▶ The window has three panes, which are (from left to right) Mailboxes/Folders, Messages, and Reading. These work just like the panes in the Mail app on an iOS device or the Mail application on a Mac. Select the mailbox or folder containing the messages you want to see. The list of messages appears in the Messages pane. Select a message to view it in the Reading pane.

▶ You can resize the panes by dragging the vertical lines that separate them.

▶ To collapse or expand the Mailbox/Folder pane, click the **triangle inside a box** icon at the top of the Messages pane.

▶ To check for new messages, click the **circled arrow** at the bottom of the Mailboxes/Folders pane.

▶ You can create new folders on the server by clicking the **Add** (**+**) button at the top of the Folders section. Name the folder and press **Return** (Mac) or **Enter** (Windows) to save it.

▶ You can move messages to a folder by dragging them from a mailbox into a folder. Any folders you create are available on any device accessing your account.

▶ You can sort messages in the Messages pane using the pop-up menu at the top. Options include Date, From, and Subject. You can also choose the sort order.

▶ Click the **Action** (gear) button to access a number of useful commands. Preferences enables you to set a number of preferences that determine how the application works; these include viewing, forwarding, where messages are saved, default settings for new messages, email rules, and the "vacation" settings to create an automatic reply to mail you receive. Other commands include Mark, which you can use to mark messages; Delete Folder, to remove folders you no longer need; Empty Trash, to permanently remove deleted messages; and Print, to print email messages.

Working with Email Aliases

One of the benefits of iCloud email is that you can have up to three email aliases. An alias is an email address that you can create that points to your iCloud account but hides your actual iCloud account/Apple ID. These are really useful for shielding your primary address, such as to protect it from spam or to have an address for a specific purpose. For example, an iCloud account name might be something like sirwilliamwallace@icloud.com. If this were my account and I wanted to promote a book I was writing, I could create an alias such as styicloud@icloud.com. When people send email to that address, it comes to the same place, although it appears to be a different address.

Aliases are really good to use in places where you are likely to get spammed, such as online shopping, forums, and so on. If an alias gets spammed, you can simply delete it, and your spam troubles are gone. You can create a replacement for it quite easily.

To create an alias, perform the following steps:

1. Open the Mail web application.

2. Click the **Action** (gear) button.

3. Choose **Preferences**.

4. Click the **Accounts** tab.

5. Click **Add an alias**. (If you have already used the maximum number of aliases, this command isn't available. You need to delete one of the existing aliases to be able to create a new one.) The Create Mail Alias sheet appears.

6. Create the alias by typing it in the **Alias** field.

7. Enter the name you want to appear as the From address in the **Full Name** field. This can be any name you want; it doesn't have to be your real name and shouldn't be if you are creating the address for protection against spam.

8. Enter a description of the alias in the **Description** field. This can be helpful to remember why you created the alias later on.

9. Click the **Label Color** to associate with the alias. When you receive messages sent to the alias, they are coded with the color you select, making it easier to know when the mail was sent to an alias as opposed to your actual iCloud address.

10. When you're ready to create the alias, as shown in Figure 9.11, click **OK**. The alias is checked to make sure no one else is using it and it doesn't violate any rules. If either of these is true, you have to change the alias until they aren't. When the alias passes inspection, you see the Mail Alias Created sheet.

11. Click **Done**. The alias is ready to use.

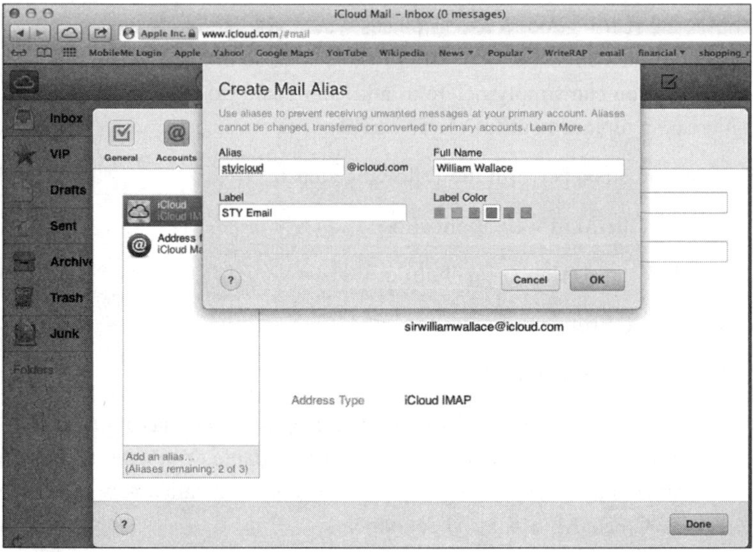

FIGURE 9.11   An alias is useful for shielding your iCloud address or for special purposes, such as promoting a book.

When someone sends email to an alias, it comes into your mailbox just like email sent to your iCloud email address. The To address is the alias, and it is color-coded as indicated. You can send email from an alias too, which is especially important in the fight against spam.

TIP: **Aliases in OS X Mail**

To administer your aliases in Mac OS X's Mail application, open its Preferences dialog box, click the **Accounts** tab, click **Account Information**, and then open the **Alias** menu. You see a number of commands you can use to work with your aliases, such as Edit Aliases, which enables you to change an alias on your iCloud website.

You can use the Addresses tab of the preferences window to also do the following:

▶ To delete an alias you no longer want, select it and click **Delete Alias**.

▶ You can also change an alias's description, name, and associated color by selecting it and using the tools that appear in the right part of the Accounts window.

▶ To temporarily disable an alias, check the **Disable this alias account** check box.

Summary

In this lesson, you learned how to use your iCloud email account on iOS devices and computers, as well as how to use the iCloud email web application. In the next lesson, you learn how to use iCloud for your contacts.

LESSON 10

Using iCloud to Manage Your Contacts

In this lesson, you learn how to use iCloud to manage your contact information on iOS devices and computers.

Using iCloud to Manage Contact Information

Using a contact manager application is a great way to keep track of the information you need to keep in touch with people by phone, email, chat, texting, tweeting, and... well, you get the idea. It's likely that you use contact information on several devices. For example, you might make phone calls and send text messages on an iPhone or email and chat using a computer.

iCloud is extremely useful in helping you keep your contact information current and available everywhere you need it, including on iOS devices, Macintosh computers, and Windows computers. After you've enabled contact syncing via iCloud, you have the same contact information available to you on each device; any changes you make on one device are automatically made on the other devices too.

iCloud contact syncing is designed to work with the following apps:

- ▶ Contacts on iOS devices
- ▶ Contacts on Macintosh computers
- ▶ Outlook on Windows computers
- ▶ Contacts on your iCloud website

Configuring iCloud for Contacts on an iOS Device

To ensure contact information is communicated to and from the cloud, you need to configure each iOS device to include contact information in the sync process. You can also change the settings that impact how contact information is displayed on your iOS devices.

Configuring iCloud Contact Syncing on an iOS Device

To include contact information on an iOS device in the sync process, perform the following steps:

1. Open the Settings app.

2. Tap **iCloud**.

3. Set the **Contacts** switch to ON, as shown in Figure 10.1. Contact information on the device is now copied to and from the cloud.

FIGURE 10.1   Setting Contacts to ON causes an iOS device to sync contact information with the cloud.

Configuring How Contacts Display on an iOS Device

On an iOS device, you can configure some aspects of how contact information is displayed in the Contacts app and other places in which contact information is displayed (such as when you look up a phone number on an iPhone). You can determine how contacts are sorted on lists (by first or last name), and you can choose which of those names appears first on lists. Configure your contact preferences by following these steps:

1. Open the Settings app.

2. Tap **Mail, Contacts, Calendars**.

3. Scroll down until you see the Contacts section, as shown in Figure 10.2.

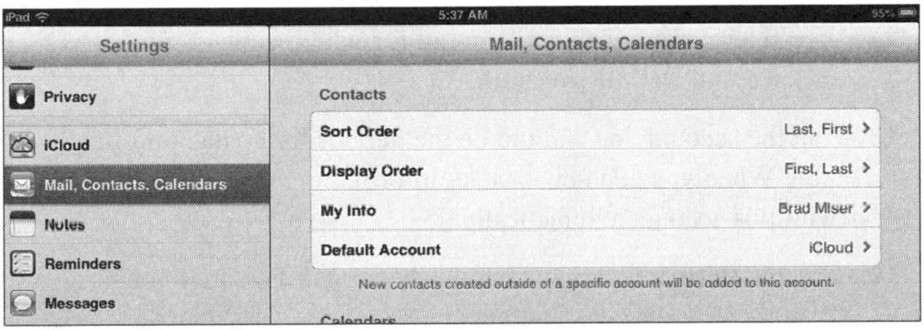

FIGURE 10.2   Use the Contacts section on the Mail, Contacts, Calendars screen to configure your contact preferences.

4. Tap **Sort Order**.

5. To have contacts sorted by first name and then last name, tap **First, Last**.

6. To have contacts sorted by last name and then first name, tap **Last, First**.

7. Tap the **Return** button, which is labeled **Mail** on an iPhone or iPod touch and **Mail, Contacts** on an iPad.

8. Tap **Display Order**.

9. To show contacts in the format "first name, last name," tap **First, Last**.

10. To show contacts in the format "last name, first name," tap **Last, First**.

11. Tap the **Return** button, which is labeled **Mail** on an iPhone or iPod touch and **Mail, Contacts** on an iPad.

12. Tap **My Info**.

13. Use the Contacts app to find and tap your contact information. This tells the device your contact information, which it can insert for you in various places. You return to the Mail, Contacts, Calendars screen and see the contact information you selected next to **My Info**.

14. If you have more than one account for which contact syncing is enabled, tap **Default Account**.

15. Tap the account you want to be the default for contact information. When you add new contact information, it is associated with this account automatically.

16. Tap the **Return** button, which is labeled **Mail** on an iPhone or iPod touch and **Mail, Contacts** on an iPad.

Configuring iCloud Contact Syncing on a Mac

You can sync contact information on a Mac by performing the following steps:

1. Open the System Preferences application.

2. Click the **iCloud** icon. The iCloud pane opens, as shown in Figure 10.3.

3. Check the **Contacts** check box.

FIGURE 10.3   When you enable contact syncing on a Mac, your contact information in Address Book is stored in the cloud.

After you've enabled contact syncing, contact information in the Contacts app is uploaded to the cloud, where it is synced to other devices. Any changes you make on any device are communicated from the device to the cloud and back to the Contacts app on the Mac.

> NOTE: **Contacts from Other Accounts**
>
> A number of services can store your contact information and can be synced on your devices, the most significant of which is Exchange. When syncing is enabled for these accounts, within the contacts application (such as Contacts on a Mac or on iOS devices), you can select specific accounts to work with the contact information stored there.

Configuring iCloud Contact Syncing on a Windows PC

On a Windows PC, you can enable contact syncing with Outlook by configuring the iCloud control panel, as described in the following steps:

1. Open the iCloud control panel.

2. Check the **Mail, Contacts, Calendars, & Tasks with Outlook** check box, as shown in Figure 10.4.

FIGURE 10.4 You can sync contact information in Outlook via your iCloud account.

3. Click **Apply**. If Outlook is open, you're prompted to close it so your contacts can be added to it. If it isn't open, you return to the iCloud control panel.

4. When you see the **Setup is complete** dialog box, click **Done**.

After you've enabled contact syncing, your iCloud contacts are available in the Outlook application, as shown in Figure 10.5.

FIGURE 10.5 Here, you see contact information from the cloud being displayed in Outlook.

Using the iCloud Contacts Web Application

On your iCloud website, you can use the Contacts web application to access your contact information from any computer that runs a supported web browser and has an Internet connection. This is convenient for those rare times when you don't have one of your other devices available to you.

To access the iCloud Contacts web application, perform the following steps:

1. Log in to your iCloud website (see Lesson 1, "Getting Started with Your iCloud Account and Website," for the details).

2. If you aren't on the Home screen that shows all the app icons, click the **cloud** button located in the upper-left corner of the screen to move there.

3. Click the **Contacts** icon. You move into the web contacts application, as shown in Figure 10.6.

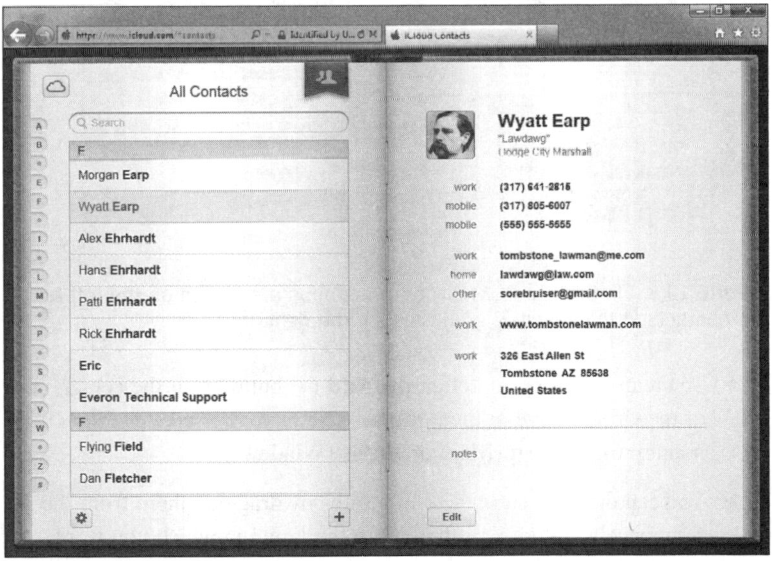

FIGURE 10.6   The Contacts app on your iCloud website simulates an address book.

> **NOTE: iCloud Contacts App Seem Familiar?**
>
> If you use the Contacts app on a Mac or on an iOS device, the web application will look familiar to you because it uses a very similar interface.

Following are some pointers about using the Contacts web application:

▶ The contacts available to you are on the left page when you see the icon with two silhouettes at the top, just to the left of the center of the "book." The name of the page is the name of the contact group with which you are working.

▶ When you click the **icon with two silhouettes**, the list of contacts moves to the right page. On the left page, you see your contact groups. When you select a group, you see the list of contacts it contains on the page on the right. You will be working with that group, as shown in Figure 10.7. To work with all your contacts, select **All Contacts**.

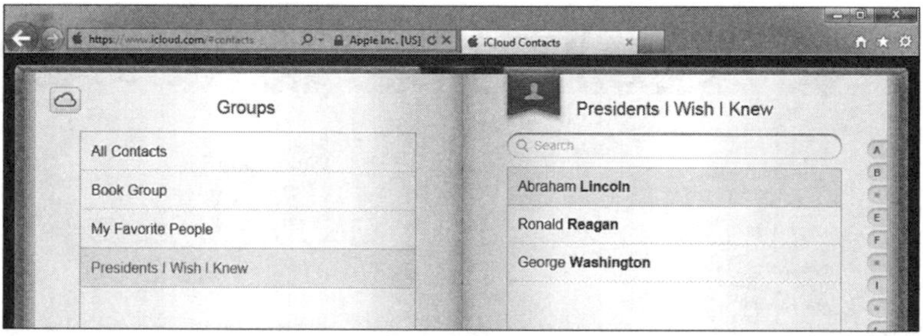

FIGURE 10.7 In this mode, your contact groups are shown on the left and the contacts in the selected group are on the right.

▶ To create a new group, click the **Add** (**+**) button near the center of the Groups page at the bottom. A new group is created. Name it and press **Return** (Mac) or **Enter** (Windows).

▶ You can then place contacts in groups by dragging them from the right page and dropping them onto the group in which you want them to be stored on the left page. In most cases, you'll be dragging contacts from the All Contacts group into other groups, but you can drag contacts from any group into another group. Contacts can be stored in more than one group at the same time.

▶ Click the **icon with one silhouette**; the list of contacts in the group you selected is shown on the left page. You can browse the list or search it by entering search information in the Search bar at the top of the window. You can click letters on the "index" along the left edge of the "book" to jump to a specific section of contacts.

▶ When you select a contact on the left page, you see detailed information for that contact on the right page.

▶ To change a contact's information, click the **Edit** button. The contact page moves into edit mode, and you can change its information. Click **Done** when you've made all the changes you want to make.

▶ To add a new contact, click the **Add** (+) button located near the middle of the bottom of the screen on which the list of contacts in the current group is displayed. Complete the resulting form to create the contact.

▶ Click the **Action** (gear) button in the lower-left corner of the screen to see a menu of additional commands.

▶ If you choose the **Preferences** command on that menu, you can set the display and format options for your contacts in the web application.

▶ Choose **Make This My Card** to select your own contact information, which is used in the other applications. This also becomes your contact information on your other devices.

▶ Choose **Refresh Contacts** to manually sync the web application with your other contact applications running on various devices.

LESSON 10: Using iCloud to Manage Your Contacts

Summary

In this lesson, you learned how to use iCloud to help you manage your contact information on iOS devices and computers as well as how to use the Contacts web application. In the next lesson, you learn how to do the same for your calendars.

LESSON 11
Using iCloud with Your Calendars

In this lesson, you learn how to use iCloud to manage your calendars on iOS devices and computers and how to use the iCloud Calendar web app.

Using iCloud to Manage Your Calendars

A calendar app is a great way to keep track of important (and even not-so-important) events in your life. Using a calendar app on a computer is useful, but having your calendars with you at all times on your iOS devices is even better because you can manage your life while you are on the move.

iCloud helps you keep your calendars current and available everywhere you need them, including on iOS devices, Macintosh computers, and Windows computers. After you've enabled calendar syncing via iCloud, you have the same calendars available to you on each device; any changes (such as creating a new event) that you make on one device are automatically available on the other devices too. You can also use the iCloud Calendar web app to access your calendars from any computer with a supported web browser and an Internet connection.

iCloud calendar syncing is designed to work with the following:

▶ Calendar app on iOS devices

▶ Calendar app on Macintosh computers

▶ Outlook on Windows computers

▶ Calendar app on your iCloud website

Configuring iCloud Calendars on an iOS Device

To ensure your calendar information is communicated to and from the cloud, you need to configure each iOS device to include calendar information in the sync process. You can also change your calendar preferences on your iOS devices.

Configuring iCloud Calendar Syncing on an iOS Device

To include calendar information on an iOS device in the sync process, perform the following steps:

1. Open the Settings app.

2. Tap **iCloud**.

3. Set the **Calendars** switch to ON, as shown in Figure 11.1. Calendar information on the device is copied to and from the cloud.

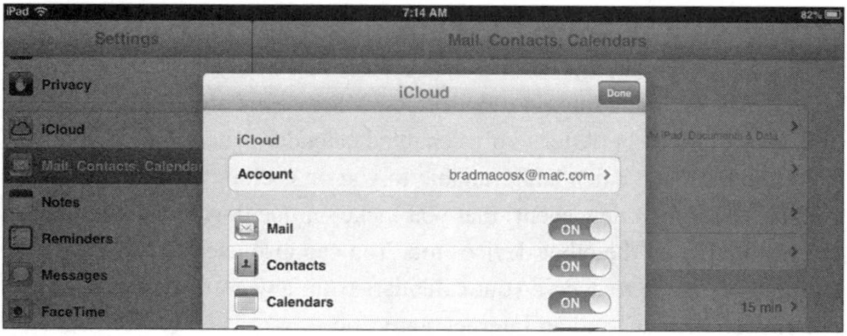

FIGURE 11.1   Setting Calendars to ON causes an iOS device to sync your calendars with the cloud.

Configuring Calendar Preferences on an iOS Device

You can change a number of aspects of how calendars work on your iOS devices. Before we jump into the steps, however, one of the Calendar app's functions requires a bit of explanation.

The Time Zone Support feature associates time zones with your events. This can be a useful thing, but it also can be a bit confusing. If Time Zone Support is enabled (ON), the iOS device displays event times according to the time zone selected on the Time Zone Support screen. (You learn about this shortly.) When Time Zone Support is disabled (OFF), the time zone used for calendars is the device's current time zone that is set automatically based on your network connection or your manual setting; this means that when you change time zones (automatically or manually), the times for calendar events shift accordingly.

For example, suppose you set Indianapolis (which is in the Eastern time zone) as the device's time zone. If you enable Time Zone Support and then set San Francisco as the time zone for Time Zone Support, the events on your calendars are shown according to the Pacific time zone because that is San Francisco's time zone rather than Eastern time (Indianapolis's time zone).

In other words, when Time Zone Support is ON, the dates and times for events become fixed based on the time zone you select for Time Zone Support. If you change the time zone the device is in, there is no change to the dates and times for events shown on the calendar because they remain set according to the Time Zone Support time zone you select.

In any case, you need to be aware of the time zone you are using for your calendars (the one you select if Time Zone Support is ON or the time zone of your current location if it is OFF) and the time zone with which events are associated.

NOTE: **Time Zone Support in Calendar Apps**

With some calendar apps (such as Calendar on a Mac), you can associate an event with a specific time zone when you schedule it. This is useful because events shift with the device's time zone; for example, if you schedule a meeting for 3 p.m. in the Eastern time zone and then travel to the Pacific time zone, the meeting moves on the calendar to reflect a 12 p.m. start time.

Configure your calendar preferences by following these steps:

1. Open the Settings app.

2. Tap **Mail, Contacts, Calendars**.

3. Scroll down until you see the Calendars section, as shown in Figure 11.2.

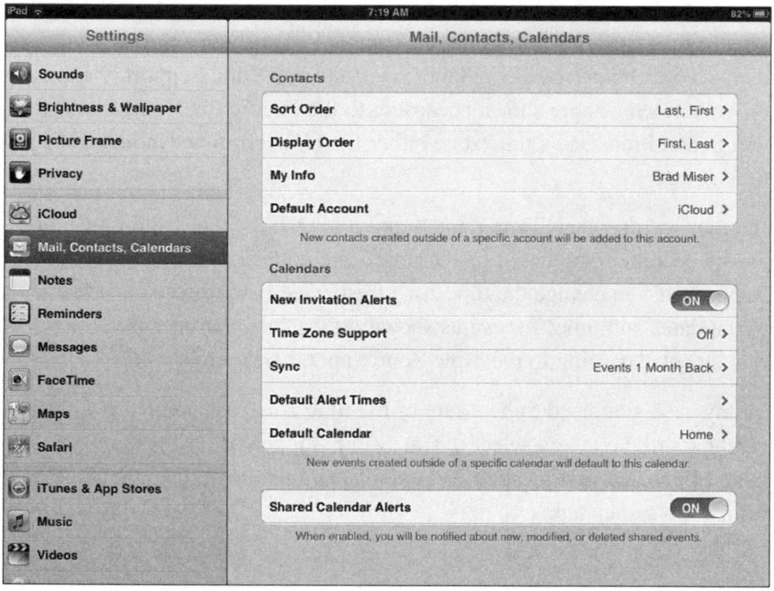

FIGURE 11.2   Use the tools in the Calendars section to configure your calendar preferences.

4. If you don't want to be alerted when you receive invitations to events, set the **New Invitation Alerts** switch to OFF. When you are invited to events, you won't see notifications. To be alerted again, tap **OFF** to toggle the status back ON.

5. Tap **Time Zone Support**.

6. To have the device display meeting and event times on its calendars based on the device's current time zone (either set automatically through the cellular network or set manually), set the **Time Zone Support** switch to OFF and skip to step 11.

7. To have event times displayed according to a specific time zone, set the **Time Zone Support** switch to ON and move to the next step.

8. Tap **Time Zone**

9. Type the name of the city you want to use to set the time zone. As you type, the Settings app lists the cities that match your search.

> NOTE: **What's in a Name?**
> The specific city you select in step 10 matters only in that it is in the time zone you want to use for your calendars. If you can't find the specific city you want to use, just choose one that is in the same time zone as the one you want to use.

10. When the city you want to use appears on the list, tap it. You move back to the Time Zone Support screen, and the city you selected is shown in the Time Zone field.

11. Tap the **Return** button, which is labeled **Mail** on an iPhone or iPod touch and **Mail, Contacts** on an iPad.

12. To set the period of time over which past events are synced, tap **Sync**.

13. Tap the amount of time you want events to be synced; tap **All Events** to have all events synced, regardless of their age. For example, if you tap **Event 1 Month Back**, your calendars in the Calendar app show events within the past month.

14. Tap the **Return** button, which is labeled **Mail** on an iPhone or iPod touch and **Mail, Contacts** on an iPad.

15. Tap **Default Alert Times**.

16. Tap the item for which you want to set a default alert time; the options are **Birthdays**, **Events**, and **All-Day Events**, as shown in Figure 11.3.

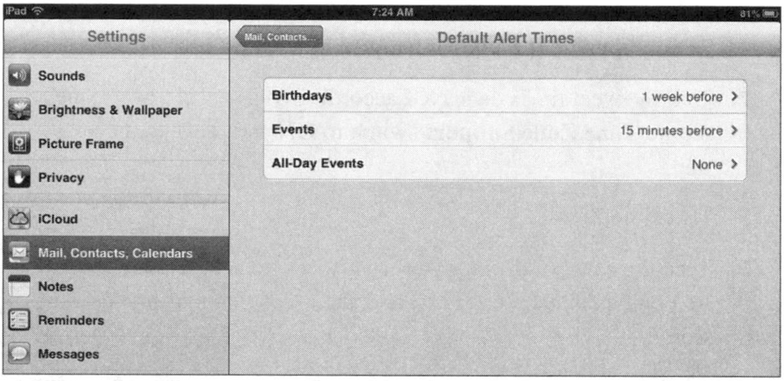

FIGURE 11.3   You can choose the default alert times for items on your calendars using this screen.

17. Tap the alert time that you want to set as the default for the type of item you tapped in step 16. For example, if you tap **Events** and then tap **30 minutes before**, when you create a new event on your device, it will have a 30-minute alert set automatically. You can change the alerts for any event so this setting just gives you a starting point.

18. Tap **Default Alert Times**.

19. Set the default alert times for the other two items using steps 16 through 18.

20. Tap the **Return** button, which is labeled **Mail** on an iPhone or iPod touch and **Mail, Contacts** on an iPad.

21. Tap **Default Calendar** (if you have only one calendar on your device, skip this and the next step). You see the list of all calendars configured on the iOS device based on its sync settings.

22. Tap the calendar that you want to be the default, meaning the one that is selected unless you specifically choose a different one. When you create a new event, you can change the calendar on which it appears; this setting only determines the initial calendar for new events.

Configuring iCloud Calendar Syncing on a Mac

You can sync calendar information on a Mac by following these steps:

1. Open the System Preferences application.

2. Click the **iCloud** icon. The iCloud pane opens, as shown in Figure 11.4.

3. Check the **Calendars & Reminders** check box.

FIGURE 11.4 When you enable calendar syncing on a Mac, your calendar information in iCloud is stored in the cloud.

After you enable calendar syncing, iCloud calendar information in the Calendar app, as shown in Figure 11.5, is uploaded to the cloud, where it is synced to other devices. Any changes you make on any device are communicated to the cloud and back to your other devices.

> NOTE: **Calendars from Other Accounts**
>
> A number of services can store your calendars and can be synced on your devices, with one of the most useful being Exchange. Within the calendar application (such as Calendar on a Mac or on iOS devices), you can select specific accounts to work with the calendar information stored there.

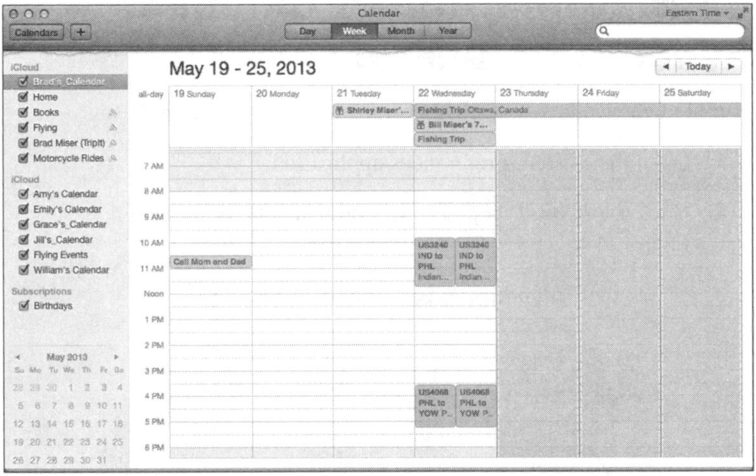

FIGURE 11.5   You can use Calendar on a Mac to display and manage your iCloud calendars.

Configuring iCloud Calendar Syncing on a Windows PC

On a Windows PC, you can enable calendar syncing with Outlook by configuring the iCloud control panel as described in the following steps:

1. If Outlook is open, close it.

2. Open the iCloud control panel.

3. Check the **Mail, Contacts, Calendars & Tasks with Outlook** check box, as shown in Figure 11.6.

4. Click **Apply**. If Outlook is open, you're prompted to close it so your calendar information can be added to it.

FIGURE 11.6 You can sync calendar information in Outlook via your iCloud account.

   5. When you see the **Setup is complete** dialog box, click **Done**.

   6. Click **Close** to close the iCloud control panel.

After you enable calendar syncing, your iCloud calendars are available in Outlook, as shown in Figure 11.7.

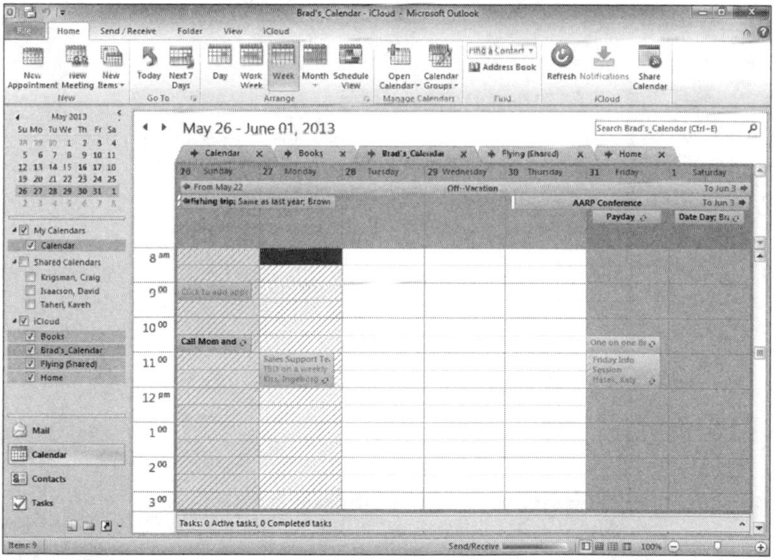

FIGURE 11.7 Here, you see calendar information from the cloud displayed in Outlook.

Using the iCloud Calendar Web App

On your iCloud website, you can use the Calendar web application to access your calendar information from any computer that runs a supported web browser and has an Internet connection. This is convenient when you don't have one of your other devices available to you.

To access the iCloud Calendar web application, perform the following steps:

1. Log in to your iCloud website (see Lesson 1, "Getting Started with Your iCloud Account and Website," for the details).

2. If you aren't on the Home page that shows icons for the various web apps, click the **cloud** button located in the upper-left corner of the window to move there.

3. Click the **Calendar** icon. You move into the web calendar app, as shown in Figure 11.8.

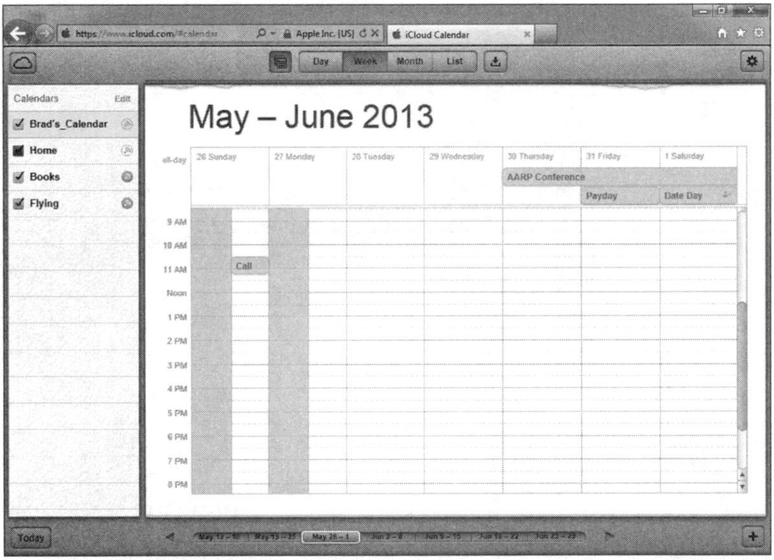

FIGURE 11.8 The Calendar application on your iCloud website enables you to manage your calendars from just about any computer.

Following are some pointers about using the Calendar web app:

▶ The calendars available to you are shown on the Calendars list on the far left pane of the window. You can show or hide the list of calendars by clicking the button just to the left of the Day button at the top of the screen. Hiding it provides more room in the window for your calendars.

▶ To show a specific calendar, check its check box. When you uncheck a calendar's check box, its events are hidden but remain unchanged. You can display them again by checking the calendar's check box.

▶ You can change how the calendar is displayed by clicking any of the following: **Day, Week, Month,** or **List**. The window changes to reflect your selection. The Day option presents calendars in a "calendar book" with each day shown on two pages; the left page shows detail for the day's events, whereas the right page shows an overview of the day. **Week** shows a full week of days, and you can probably guess what clicking the **Month** button shows. The **List** option includes two panes: The left pane shows a month-at-a-glance view, and the right pane shows detail for the selected day.

▶ To work with invitations or other calendar notifications you have received, click the button just to the right of the List button; this button has a badge showing how many new notifications you have. Use the resulting window to work with your notifications, such as to accept an invitation to a meeting.

▶ Change the timeframe shown on the calendar using the scroll bar and arrows at the bottom of the window. This shows the context of the view currently selected; for example, when the Week view is selected, you see buttons that represent weeks.

▶ To create an event, click the **Add** (+) button located in the bottom-right corner of the window. Use the resulting dialog box to record the event's details, including name, location, and other details. Click **OK** to create the event on the selected calendar.

▶ Open the Action menu by clicking the **gear** button in the upper-right corner of the window. You see a number of useful commands, including Preferences, New Event, New Calendar, Delete Event, Go to Today, Go to Date, and Show Declined Events.

NOTE: **Reminders**

Reminders are notifications you can set to remind you of just about anything. You can manage your reminders in the Reminders app on Macs and iOS devices or in Outlook on Windows PCs (reminders are called "tasks" in Outlook). You learn more about reminders in Lesson 12, "Using iCloud to Sync Other Information."

Summary

In this lesson, you learned how to use iCloud to help you manage your calendars on iOS devices and computers as well as how to use the Calendar web app. In the next lesson, you learn how to use iCloud to sync other kinds of information, such as your bookmarks, notes, and reminders.

LESSON 12

Using iCloud to Sync Other Information

In this lesson, you learn how to include bookmarks, notes, and reminders in your iCloud syncs so that you can share these items on all your devices.

Understanding Other Sync Options

In the previous lessons, you learned about the "more important" sync options, which include email, calendars, and contacts. In this lesson, you learn about other sync options that are also very useful. These include the following:

▶ **Reminders**—Reminders (called "tasks" in Outlook) can be just about anything you want to be reminded about. You can enter the text for a reminder and then configure how, where, and when you want to be reminded about the "thing." Of course, reminders can be for tasks that you need to do and are just as useful, if not more useful, for general information, such as something you want to remember. On Macs and iOS devices, you use the Reminders app to manage reminders, and on Windows PCs, you manage reminders (tasks) in Outlook.

▶ **Bookmarks**—You can use this feature to ensure you have the same set of bookmarks in your web browser on any device. On iOS devices and Macs, synced bookmarks are available in Safari, and on a Windows PC, they are available in Internet Explorer or Safari.

▶ **Notes**—These are text "snippets" that can capture any text you want. To work with notes on an iOS device or Mac, you use the Notes app. On a Windows PC, you currently can't sync notes via iCloud. However, another way to sync is explained later in this lesson.

Configuring Other Sync Options on an iOS Device

To configure any of the previously mentioned sync options on an iOS device, perform the following steps:

1. Open the Settings app.

2. Tap **iCloud**. The iCloud settings screen opens, as shown in Figure 12.1.

FIGURE 12.1   You can also include reminders, bookmarks, and notes in your iCloud syncs on iOS devices.

3. To include reminders in your syncs, set the **Reminders** switch to
    ON.

4. To include your Safari bookmarks in your syncs, set the **Safari**
    switch to ON.

5. To do the same for your notes, set the **Notes** switch to ON.

After you've enabled these options, work with them in the following apps:

► Use the Reminders app to view, create, and manage your
  reminders. You can include a number of elements in your
  reminders, such as notes, priorities, and so on, as shown in
  Figure 12.2. On an iPhone, you can even trigger reminders based
  on your location, such as when you arrive or leave a specific
  location.

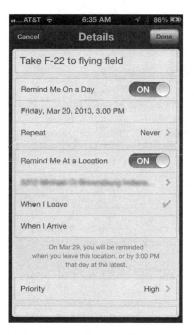

FIGURE 12.2   Reminders on an iPhone can even be triggered by location
changes in addition to specific times and dates.

▶ You can use your bookmarks in the Safari app.

▶ To work with notes, use the Notes app. You can create multiple notes; you can copy and paste content to and from the Notes app in addition to typing it in. On an iPhone 4S or newer, you can use the dictation feature to speak the notes you want to capture.

Configuring Other Sync Options on a Mac

To set up these sync options on a Mac, do the following:

1. Open the iCloud pane of the System Preferences, as shown in Figure 12.3.

FIGURE 12.3 Use the iCloud pane of the System Preferences application to configure your additional sync options on a Mac.

2. To sync your reminders, check the **Calendars & Reminders** check box.

3. To sync your notes, ensure the **Notes** check box is checked.

4. To sync your bookmarks, check the **Safari** check box.

To work with your synced information, use the following applications:

▶ Use the Notes app to work with your notes. The Notes app enables you to read, change, or delete existing notes or to create new ones. Any changes you make in the Notes app are updated on the cloud and on any other devices on which notes are synced.

▶ Use the Reminders app to manage your reminders. Like the Reminders app on an iOS device, you can have multiple lists of reminders. Any changes you make to the reminders on your Mac are communicated to the cloud and to all the other devices with which your reminders are synced.

▶ Your synced bookmarks are available in the Safari web browser.

Configuring Other Sync Options on a Windows PC

To configure these sync options on a Windows PC, perform the following steps:

1. Open the iCloud control panel, as shown in Figure 12.4.

FIGURE 12.4   Use the iCloud control panel to configure your additional sync options on a Windows PC.

2. To sync your reminders, check the **Mail, Contacts, Calendars, & Tasks with Outlook** check box.

3. To sync your bookmarks, check the **Bookmarks with *browser*** check box, where *browser* is the currently selected web browser.

4. Click the **Options** button. (You only see the Options button if both Safari and Internet Explorer are installed on your computer.)

5. Select the web browser in which you want to use your synced bookmarks. The options are Internet Explorer and Safari.

6. Click **OK**.

7. Click **Apply**.

To access these items, use the following applications:

▶ In Outlook, reminders are called "tasks." Open Outlook and click the Tasks option. In the iCloud section, you see the reminders that have been synced via iCloud. You can open and edit the tasks (reminders) you see, as shown in Figure 12.5. To create a new task on iCloud, select the reminder list in which you want the reminder created and click New Task. (The first time you create a task, you must supply your iCloud password.)

▶ To use your synced bookmarks, use the web browser you selected in step 5.

TIP: Syncing Notes on a Windows PC

On a Windows PC, you can't currently use iCloud to sync notes. However, you can sync notes with iOS devices using iTunes. Connect the iOS device to your computer and click the device's button located in the upper-right corner of the iTunes window (if more than one device is connected to your computer, open the devices menu and select the device you want to configure). Click the **Info** tab. Check the **Sync notes with** check box and choose the application with which you want the notes synced in the drop-down list. When you sync the device, your notes move to and from the application you selected. When your notes are on the iOS device, they get synced via iCloud to other devices. However, you have to manually sync a device to get your notes on a Windows PC.

FIGURE 12.5 Here, you see a task in Outlook that was created in the Reminders app on an iPhone (refer to Figure 12.2).

Summary

In this lesson, you learned how to include bookmarks, notes, and reminders in your syncs. In the next lesson, you learn how to use iCloud to safeguard your devices and data.

LESSON 13

Using iCloud to Locate and Secure Your Devices

In this lesson, you learn how to use iCloud to locate missing devices and to protect their data.

Using iCloud to Find Devices

iOS devices are mobile; they can easily go anywhere because they are small and lightweight. They are also powerful and can store all kinds of sensitive data, from contacts to personal information you use for financial activity and other sensitive content. These two factors make the devices extremely useful. However, this also means that if you lose control of a device, bad things can happen. At worst, someone could compromise your data to steal your identity or take money from you.

Laptop computers present a similar risk. Although not quite as mobile as an iOS device, laptops can also become separated from their owners in a number of ways, from simply being misplaced to getting stolen.

iCloud includes the Find My *Device* application, where *Device* can be an iPad, iPod, iPhone, or Mac. This feature enables you to locate a device remotely. When the device is located, you can lock it, or if you feel you have lost control of it, you can erase its memory.

To use this feature, you must first enable it on each device. After it's enabled, you can locate and secure devices through your iCloud website.

NOTE: **No Find My PC**

You might have noticed that I did not mention a Windows PC on the list of devices you can find via iCloud. This feature only supports Apple devices; Windows PCs are not supported. Therefore, you'll need to find some other way to accomplish these tasks for your Windows PCs. If you use a mobile Windows PC, perform a web search to preyproject.com options that may be useful for you (one example is at www.preyproject.com).

Finding iOS Devices

Finding iOS devices via iCloud requires that you set up each device to use this feature. When that is done, you can use the Find My *Device* app on your iCloud website to locate a device, and then you can perform several different actions to secure it.

Enabling Find My iPhone on iOS Devices

To enable an iOS device to be found, perform the following steps:

1. On the Settings screen, tap **iCloud**.

2. If OFF is displayed next to **Find My *Device***, where *Device* is iPad, iPhone, or iPod, tap the switch to set it in the ON position; if ON is displayed, skip the rest of these steps.

3. Tap **Allow** at the prompt.

4. If prompted, enable **Location Services**. The Find My *Device* feature becomes active, as shown in Figure 13.1, and iCloud starts tracking the location of the device.

NOTE: **Location Services**

Find My *Device* works through the Location Services feature of iOS devices. A device can be located based on its Internet connection via a Wi-Fi or cellular Internet connection or via GPS. GPS location is most accurate, but not all iOS devices support GPS functionality.

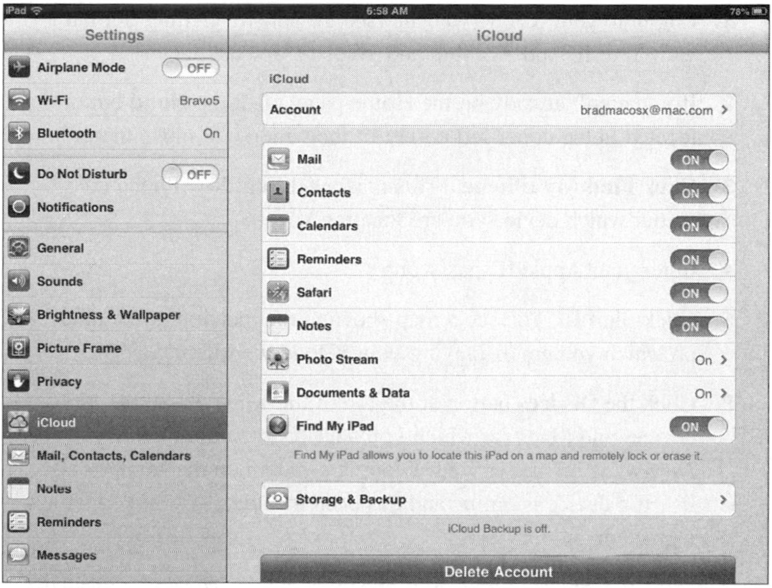

FIGURE 13.1 With Find My iPad enabled, this device can be tracked via the iCloud website.

NOTE: **Passcode**

A passcode is a four-digit number (simple) or longer string of characters (complex) that must be entered to unlock an iOS device. You should configure and use a passcode on your devices if there is any chance they can get out of your control. Without the correct passcode being entered, the device can't be unlocked, so it can't be used. Thus, your data is protected. To configure a passcode, open the Settings app. Tap **General** and then tap **Passcode Lock**. From there, you can choose the type of passcode you want and configure it. When you've done that, the passcode is required each time you unlock the device.

Using Find My iPhone with iOS Devices

When the Find My *Device* feature is activated, you can access your device's location via your iCloud website by doing the following tasks:

1. Log in to your iCloud website (see Lesson 1, "Getting Started with Your iCloud Account and Website" for the details).

2. If you aren't already on the Home page, click the **cloud** button located in the upper-left corner of the window to move there.

3. Click **Find My iPhone**. (This is labeled Find My iPhone no matter which device you are locating.)

4. Enter your Apple ID password.

5. Click **Sign In**. You see a map showing the location of the device on which you are displaying your iCloud website.

6. Click the **Devices** button at the top of the window. All the iOS devices and Macs for which you have enabled the Find My *Device* feature under your iCloud are shown on the My Devices list. If a device is online and has been located, it is marked with a green dot.

7. Click the device you want to locate. If the device can be located, you see it on a map. You also see a dialog that shows you the options you have to find the device, as shown in Figure 13.2 and explained in the following paragraphs.

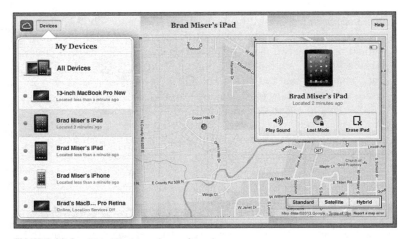

FIGURE 13.2   This iPad has been found.

When you have located a device, you can perform the following actions:

▶ **Play a sound**—This does just what it sounds like. A sound is played on the device and an alert appears on its screen. This provides information to whomever has the device—such as if you've loaned the device to someone and want it back. The sound can help you locate the device if it is in the same general vicinity as you.

▶ **Lost Mode**—This does locks the device so it can't be used. If your device doesn't already have a passcode, you create one when you lock it. This can protect your device without changing its data. You can also display contact information on the device's screen to enable someone to get in touch with you.

▶ **Erase**—This erases the device's memory as the "last chance" to protect your data. You should only do this in the worst-case scenario because when you erase the device, you lose the ability to find it again.

NOTE: **Keeping You Informed**

Whenever you use one of the Find My iPhone functions, such as playing a sound or using the Lost mode, you receive emails to your iCloud email account showing the action taken along with the device, date, and time on which it was performed. You may also receive messages through the Messages app on iOS devices.

Each of these actions is explained in the following steps.

Here's how to send a sound or message to an iOS device:

1. Locate the device as described in the previous steps.

2. Click **Play Sound**. The sound plays on the device and an alert message appears on the screen.

NOTE: **The Sound Remains the Same**

When you send a sound to a device you are finding, it plays even if the device is muted.

To stop the sound from playing on the device, unlock it and tap the **OK** button on the message prompt (if it isn't locked, you can just tap the **OK** button on the alert). (If you don't require a passcode, anyone who has the phone can do this, which is one reason requiring a passcode is more secure.)

To prevent someone from using a device, you can lock it remotely by doing the following:

1. Locate the device using the earlier steps.

2. Click **Lost Mode**. What happens next depends on whether or not the device has a passcode.

3. If the device currently has a passcode, skip to step 6.

4. If you haven't entered a passcode on the device (which you should have, per the earlier Note), you're prompted to create one by entering it (see Figure 13.3).

FIGURE 13.3   Ideally, you would have already created a passcode on your device, but if you haven't, you can do so when you put the device into Lost mode.

5. Re-enter it at the prompt.

6. If you want to send a phone number to the device so that someone can call you about it, enter it at the prompt.

7. Click **Next**.

8. Enter the message you want to appear on the device (see Figure 13.4). This can be your request that whoever has the device call you, instructions for returning the device, and so on.

Cancel   **Lost Mode**   Done

Enter a message that will be shown with your phone number on your iPhone.

I've misplaced my iPhone. I would appreciate a phone call to let me know where it is. A reward will be provided. Brad Miser|

FIGURE 13.4   This message is displayed on the device's screen when it enters Lost mode.

9. Tap **Done**.

When the device enters Lost mode, it is locked and protected with the existing passcode or the new one you created during the Lost mode process. The phone number and message you entered appears on the device's screen, as shown in Figure 13.5. If the device is an iPhone, the person finding it can tap the Call button to call the number you entered.

The device remains in Lost mode until it is unlocked.

> **NOTE: Auto-Lock**
>
> The Auto-Lock feature causes an iOS device to automatically lock after a specific period of inactive time has passed. If you protect your iOS device with a passcode, you should also set the Auto-Lock. After the inactive time passes, the device locks, and the passcode is required to unlock it. This minimizes the time during which the device is vulnerable if you lose control of it. To set the Auto-Lock, open the Settings app. Tap **General** and then tap **Auto-Lock**.

FIGURE 13.5   Hopefully, someone will return my iPhone!

If you decide you've lost control of your device and want to protect the information it contains, take the following steps:

1. Locate the device using the earlier steps.

2. Click **Erase** *Device*, where *Device* is the type of device you've found.

CAUTION: **Wiping a Device**

When you wipe a device, all its data is deleted, and it is reset to factory conditions. This means you will no longer be able to use Find My iPhone to locate it. Only do this when you're pretty sure the device is out of your control or that you won't be getting it back any time soon.

---

3. Click **Erase**.

4. Enter your Apple ID password, as shown in Figure 13.6.

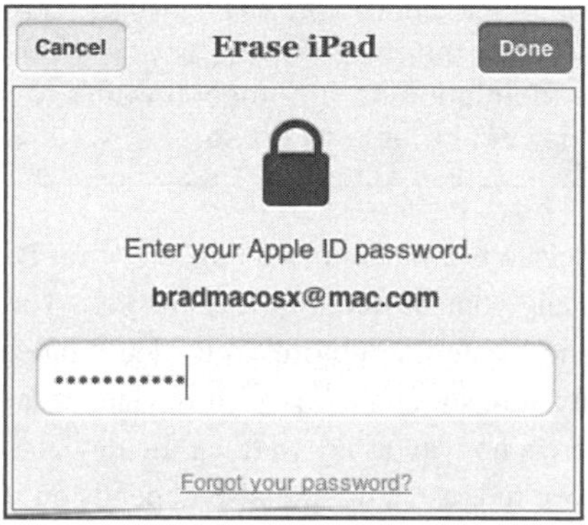

FIGURE 13.6 When all hope of a quick recovery is lost, erase a device to protect its data.

5. Click **Done**. All the data on your device is erased, and it is restored to factory settings.

Here are a few more tidbits to facilitate finding your devices:

▶ To update the locations of your devices, refresh the web page and reopen the My Devices list.

▶ If you lose control of your device, use an escalation of steps to try to regain control. Look at the device's location on the map. If the device appears to be near your current location, play the sound because it might help you find it again. If the device doesn't appear to be near your current location or it appears to be but you can't find it, put it in Lost mode. This will hopefully prevent someone else from using it while you locate it and allow someone who finds it to contact you. If you lose all hope of finding it again, you can erase the device to delete the data it contains. This is a severe action, so you don't want to do it prematurely.

TIP: **What Message to Send?**
When you send a message to a device that is in Lost mode, you might want to include additional contact information in the message, such as your name and where you are currently located. You could also offer a reward for the return of the device if you wanted to. Include enough information so if someone wants to return the device to you, they will be able to do so.

▶ Erasing a device is a bit of a two-edged sword. It protects your data by erasing your device, but it also means you can't use Find My iPhone to locate it anymore. You should only use this if you're pretty sure someone has your device, because after you erase it, there's no way to try to track the device's location. How fast you move to erase a device also depends on if you've required a passcode. If you do require a passcode, you know your device's data can't be accessed without that code, so it will take some time for a miscreant to crack it, and you might be slower on the erase trigger. If your device doesn't have a passcode, you might want to pull the trigger faster. If you do recover your device after it has been erased, go through the restore process using iTunes to return your device to its condition as of your most recent backup.

▶ As you use Find My iPhone, you receive email notifications about various events, such as when a device is locked, when a message you sent is displayed, and so on. These are a good way to know something about what is happening with your device, even though you might not be able to see the device for yourself.

▶ If Find My iPhone can't currently find a device, you can still initiate the same actions as when the device is found, although they won't actually happen until the device becomes visible again. To be notified when this happens, check the **Email me when this** *device* **is found** check box. When the device becomes visible to Find My iPhone, you receive an email and then can take appropriate action to locate and secure it.

▶ The circle around a device's dot indicates how precise its location is. The larger the circle, the less precise the device's location is.

▶ There's an app for that. You can download and use the free Find My iPhone app on an iOS device to use this feature. For example, you can use this app on an iPhone to locate an iPad.

CAUTION: **No Security Is Perfect**

Even with passcodes, Auto-Lock, and the Find My iPhone feature, your information stored on an iOS device can be compromised. For example, if you don't have a passcode, someone can easily disable the device's network connections, thus eliminating your ability to find it. While it's disconnected, someone can access the device's data. However, these features require that someone trying to gain access to your information be much more sophisticated to be able to do so (than if you do not use these features). This will be beyond the technical capabilities of the average hack. However, any sensitive data stored on a device (mobile or otherwise) presents some level of risk to you because no security approach is able to provide perfect protection; the goal is to use some simple and easy techniques to make compromising your data as difficult as possible.

Finding Macs

If you use a Mac, you might want to be able to locate it. Although the need for this is more obvious for a Mac laptop, it could potentially be useful if a desktop unexpectedly changes locations.

Enabling Find My Mac

To enable Find My Mac, perform the following steps:

1. Open the iCloud pane of the System Preferences application.

2. Check the **Find My Mac** check box.

3. Click **Allow** at the prompt. You can locate your Mac via the Find My iPhone application on your iCloud website or by using the Find My iPhone app on an iOS device.

Finding a Mac

To locate a Mac, perform the following steps:

1. Log in to your iCloud website (see Lesson 1 for the details).

2. If you aren't already at the Home page, click the **cloud** button in the upper-left corner to move there.

3. Click **Find My iPhone**. (This is labeled "Find My iPhone" no matter which device you are locating.)

4. Enter your Apple ID password.

5. Click **Sign In**. You see a map showing the location of the device on which you are displaying your iCloud website.

6. Click the **Devices** button at the top of the window. All the iOS devices and Macs for which you have enabled the Find My *Device* feature under your iCloud are shown on the My Devices list. If a device is online and has been located, it is marked with a green dot.

7. Click the Mac you want to locate. If it can be located, you see it on a map. You also see a dialog box that shows you the options you have to find the device, as shown in Figure 13.7.

When you locate a Mac, you can play a sound, lock it, or wipe it. These actions work similarly to those for an iOS device. See the section, "Using Find My iPhone with iOS Devices," for the details.

FIGURE 13.7   A Mac has been found!

Summary

In this lesson, you learned how to use iCloud to protect your devices. In the next lesson, you learn how to back up and restore your devices.

Using iCloud to Back Up and Restore Devices

In this lesson, you learn how to protect the data on your iOS devices by backing them up. You also learn how to restore a device from your backup and how to manage your iCloud storage space.

Backing Up iOS Devices

Your iOS devices have lots of data on them, such as photos you've taken, contacts, apps, Home screen customizations, and so on. Although it's likely you have some of this data stored elsewhere (for example, if you enabled iCloud Contacts on all your devices, your contact information is also stored on a computer), it would be a nuisance to have to redo your iOS device's configuration should something happen to it. In some cases, such as photos you've just taken, data may only be stored on the device for a period of time, and if something happens to that data during that period, it could be lost. By backing up your iOS device, you can easily restore it to recover your data and customized configuration when you need to.

Understanding Backup Options

When it comes to backing up your iOS device, you have the following two options:

> ▶ **On your computer**—You can choose to store your backup data on the computer with which you sync the device using iTunes.

There aren't many benefits to this option, but it does save space in the cloud if you store lots of other data there. And, you are likely to have a lot more space on your computer than on the cloud. However, this option has a number of disadvantages. Backups happen only when you connect the device to your computer (via USB or Wi-Fi), so your backup is only as current as the most recent sync. Also, your backup is associated with a specific computer; should something happen to that computer, your backup could be lost.

▶ **On the cloud**—You can store your backup on the cloud. This has a number of benefits. The most important is that backups can happen any time a device has access to the Internet; you aren't limited to syncing with a specific computer as you are when you back up there. For example, if you are traveling with only your iOS device, it still gets backed up automatically. The downside of using the cloud for backup is that less space is available, so only your "important" data is backed up.

The good news is that you can use both of these options. You can configure your iOS devices to use the cloud for regular, automatic backups and to periodically and manually back up your device to your computer. This approach ensures that you have the most important data backed up frequently, and you are able to restore all the data on your device if you need to (as long as your manual backups to the computer are relatively current of course).

Because this is the recommended strategy for backing up your iOS device, the rest of this chapter shows you how to configure and use backups with this approach.

Configuring an iOS Device to Back Up to the Cloud

You can determine where an iOS device is backed up either via iTunes or on the device itself.

To use iTunes to set the iCloud backup method for an iOS device, perform the following steps:

1. Connect the device to your computer and launch iTunes if it isn't open already.

2. Click the *Device* button, where *Device* is the type of device; if you have more than one device connected to iTunes, click **X Devices**, where *X* is the number of connected devices, and then click the device you want to configure on the resulting menu.

3. Click the **Summary** tab.

4. Click **iCloud**, as shown in Figure 14.1.

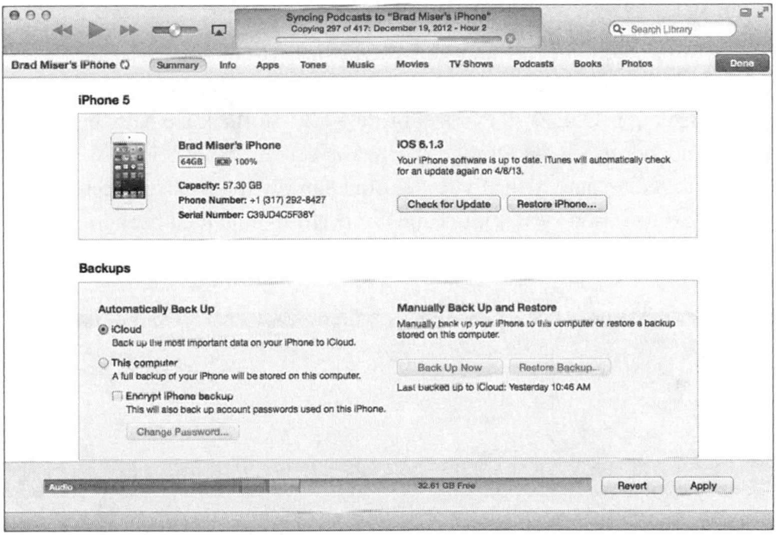

FIGURE 14.1 Click the iCloud button and then Apply to configure an iOS device to back up to the cloud.

5. Click **Apply**. The device is synced according to the current settings and is backed up to your cloud.

> TIP: **Backing Up to Computer Only**
>
> If you don't want to use iCloud for backing up, in step 4, click **This computer** instead. Backups happen only when the device is connected to iTunes (via USB cable) and synced.

To configure the cloud as the back up location directly on the device, follow these steps:

1. Open the Settings app.

2. Tap **iCloud**.

3. Tap **Storage & Backup**.

4. Set the **iCloud Backup** switch to the ON position.

5. At the prompt explaining that the device will no longer be backed up to the computer automatically, tap **OK**. When iCloud Backup is ON, as shown in Figure 14.2, the Back Up Now button appears on the Storage & Backup screen. Your device is backed up automatically to the cloud and will be backed up the next time you sync with iTunes or perform a manual backup (explained in the next section).

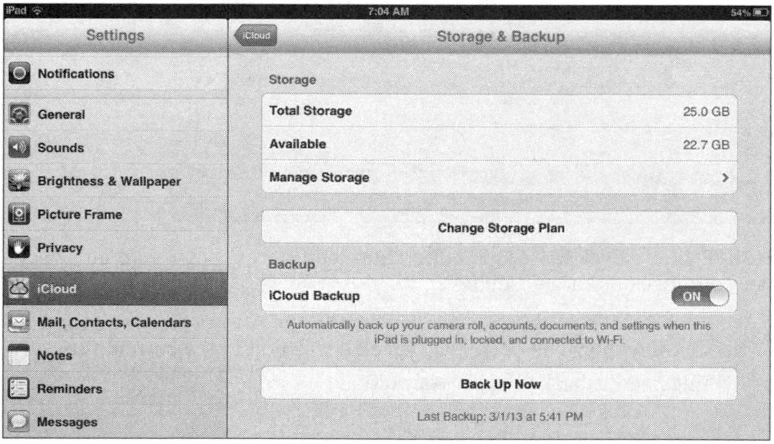

FIGURE 14.2   This device is being automatically backed up to the cloud.

Backing Up an iOS Device

When an iOS device is configured to back up to the cloud, backups happen automatically (when the device is connected to the Internet via Wi-Fi, plugged into a charger, and locked), so there's nothing you need to do to back up the device (except ensure those conditions are met). However, you can manually back up a device to the cloud to ensure your backup is current. You should also periodically back up the device to a computer to ensure you have all of its data backed up.

To back up an iOS device to the cloud at any time, perform the following steps:

1. Open the Settings app and tap **iCloud**.

2. Tap **Storage & Backup**.

3. Tap **Back Up Now**. The backup process starts and you see progress information about the backup, as shown in Figure 14.3; you can use the device for other tasks while it is being backed up. The amount of time the process takes depends on the amount of data that needs to be backed up.

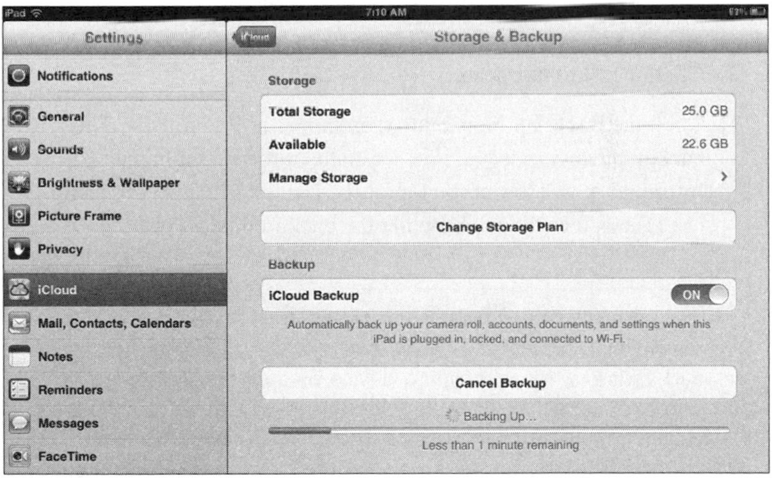

FIGURE 14.3 The important data on this device is being backed up on the cloud.

NOTE: **Important Data**

When you back up an iOS device to the cloud, only its important data is backed up. Important data includes your camera roll, accounts, documents, and settings. Music, books, and other similar items are not backed up because it is assumed those items are either available from one of the stores (iTunes, App, and so on) or stored in your iTunes Library on a computer.

Periodically, you should also manually back up the device to a computer. This ensures all its data is stored on the computer, so you can do a full restore on the device (instead of restoring just the important data from the iCloud backup).

To manually back up an iOS device to a computer, do the following:

1. Connect the device to your computer and launch iTunes, if it isn't open already.

2. Click the *Device* button, where *Device* is the type of device. Alternatively, if you have more than one device connected to iTunes, click *X* **Devices**, where *X* is the number of connected devices, and then click the device you want to configure on the resulting menu.

3. Click the **Summary** tab.

4. Click the **Back Up Now** button, as shown in Figure 14.4. The backup process runs and you see status information in the Information window at the top of the iTunes window. You can use iTunes for other tasks while the backup process occurs.

CAUTION: **No Backup When Wi-Fi Syncing**

When you sync a device over a Wi-Fi network, a backup is not included as it is when you sync a device by connecting it to a computer. To back up when the device is connected via Wi-Fi, move to the Summary screen for the device and click the **Back Up Now** button.

FIGURE 14.4 Manually back up your iOS devices to a computer so you can recover all the data on them if needed.

Restoring iOS Devices from a Backup

If you never have any problems with an iOS device or never have the need to restore it for any other reason, you don't need the information in this section. (If only life were that good!) However, you might at some point (actually rarely) need to restore an iOS device to solve a problem you are experiencing. As part of the restore process, you can choose to restore from your backup so that when the device is restored, it is in exactly the same state as it was when the backup was last performed (minus any problems you were experiencing, hopefully).

When you restore a device, you can choose to restore its software or just restore the data from a backup. If you are only having problems with data, such as missing data that you used to have, and the device is working fine, you can restore the data from the most recent backup (explained in the next section). If you are having problems with the device, such as odd behavior or errors, you should restore both its software and data (explained in the section "Restoring iOS Software and Data on iOS Devices from a Backup").

Restoring Data on iOS Devices from a Backup

If your only problem is that you've lost data from a device, you can recover data from your backup (if the device is not working correctly, you need to restore its software too, which is covered in the next section). To restore the data on an iOS device from your backup, perform the following steps:

1. Connect the device to your computer via the USB cable and launch iTunes if it isn't open already.

2. Click the *Device* button, where *Device* is the type of device. Alternatively, if you have more than one device connected to iTunes, click *X* **Devices**, where *X* is the number of connected devices, and then click the device on which you want to recover data on the resulting menu.

3. Click the **Summary** tab.

4. Click the **Restore Backup** button.

5. On the menu, select the backup containing the data you want to restore to the device (this is named with the device's name). In Figure 14.5, I've selected the name of my iPhone, so data from its backup is restored to the device.

6. Click **Restore**. The restore process begins, and you see progress information on the computer's screen and on the device's screen. When the restore is complete, the device has the data that was current as of the latest backup.

FIGURE 14.5 You can easily restore the data on your iOS device from the backup stored on your computer.

Restoring iOS Software and Data on iOS Devices from a Backup

When you have problems with a device, you can restore its software and also restore its data from the most recent backup. (If you aren't having problems with a device, but only need to recover data you've lost, use the information in the previous section instead.)

To restore a device's software and recover data from your backup, perform the following steps:

> CAUTION: **Avoid Data Loss**
>
> When you restore an iOS device, all its data is erased. If you don't have data backed up, it is lost when the restore occurs. In almost all cases, the backup is refreshed before the restore process starts. However, if that doesn't happen for some reason, perform a manual backup (if you can) before restoring the device.

1. Connect the device to your computer via the USB cable and launch iTunes if it isn't open already.

2. Click the *Device* button, where *Device* is the type of device. Alternatively, if you have more than one device connected to iTunes, click *X* **Devices**, where *X* is the number of connected devices, and then click the device on which you want to recover data on the resulting menu.

3. Click the **Summary** tab.

4. Click **Restore** or **Restore and Update** (if there are software updates available). The current version of the iOS software is downloaded to the computer (if it hasn't already been downloaded, which happens automatically when iTunes finds an update) and extracted. The restore process begins. During the restore process, you see various status changes in iTunes (such as the device disappearing from iTunes for a time) along with screen changes on the device (such as the Connect to iTunes or software install progress). You don't need to take any action during this time; iTunes prompts you when your action is required. You can use the computer (including iTunes) for other tasks during this process. Some prompts are informational; click **OK** to close them or just ignore them, and they clear in around 10 seconds. When the software installation process is complete, you see the Set Up screen.

5. Ensure the **Restore from the backup of** radio button is selected (it is the default).

6. If you don't want to restore from the most recent backup for some reason, select the version of the backup you do want to restore from on the menu. It is rare to restore from something other than the most recent backup, but you do have that option available to you.

7. Click **Continue**. Data from your backup is copied onto the device. This includes all your settings (such as syncs, Home screen customization, and so on), photos, and so on. As the process continues, you see its progress in the restore progress window. When the process is complete, a dialog box appears informing you of this. You can ignore it or click **OK** to clear it. The device restarts and is synced. When the sync finishes, the device should be in the same configuration and have the same data as it did as of the time and date of the most recent backup (or as of the time and date of an earlier backup if you selected one in step 6).

TIP: **When Did I Back Up?**

You can see the data and time of your most recent backup in a couple of places. When a device is connected to iTunes (using a cable or over a Wi-Fi network), open the **Summary** tab and look in the Manually Back Up and Restore section. Here, you see the time and date of the most recent backup to the cloud. Click the **This computer** button and you see the time and date when the device was most recently backed up to the computer (make sure you don't save changes when you move off the screen unless you want to switch the automatic backup to be done on the computer). Alternatively, open the Storage & Backup screen on the device; the date and time of the most recent backup is shown just below the Back Up Now button.

Managing Your iCloud Storage Space

Your iCloud account includes 5GB of online storage space by default. This space is used to store a number of things, including email, documents, and your iOS device backups. Music, apps, books, and other content you purchase from the iTunes Store or music you are storing on the cloud, via iTunes Match, does not count against your storage space.

To see how your space is being used, open the Settings app, tap **iCloud**, and then tap **Storage & Backup**. In the Storage section, you see the total storage space for your iCloud account and the amount of space available. If you don't store a lot of documents on your devices, it's likely that the 5GB of space is sufficient for you; it is plenty for your backups.

If you are nearing the limit of your space (the available amount is small), you can remove data by tapping **Manage Storage** and deleting items you don't need any more, which frees up space for your account. You can also upgrade the amount of space available to you by tapping the **Change Storage Plan** button. More information about managing your online storage space is provided in Lesson 1, "Getting Started with Your iCloud Account and Website."

Summary

In this lesson, you learned how to protect the data on your iOS devices by backing them up; you also learned how to restore a device from your backup and how to manage your iCloud storage space.

Index

Q-R

W-X-Y-Z

wallpaper, setting Photo Stream
  photos as, 94
web apps, 18-20
    Calendar, 198-200
    iCloud Contacts web app,
      185-187
    iCloud Mail web app, 173-174
web browser compatibility, 16-17
websites
    appleid.apple.com, 14
    iCloud website
        compatible browsers,
          16-17
        logging in to, 17
        web applications, 18-20
    My Apple ID website, 13
Windows PCs
    adding to iTunes Match, 83-84
    calendar syncing, 196-197
    compatibility with iCloud, 9
    configuring iCloud on, 47-51
    contact syncing, 183-184
    downloading iTunes Store
      purchases on, 70-71
    iCloud control panel,
      installing, 45
    iCloud email configuration,
      169-172
    listening to iTunes Match
      music, 84-85
    logging in to iCloud account
      from, 46
    manual document syncing,
      149-151

Photo Stream
    accepting shared photos,
      123-124
    enabling, 117-118
    sharing photos, 120-123
    viewing photos, 118-120
sync options, 205-207
wiping devices, 213

SamsTeachYourself

from Sams Publishing

Sams **Teach Yourself in 10 Minutes** offers straightforward, practical answers for fast results.

These small books of 250 pages or less offer tips that point out shortcuts and solutions, cautions that help you avoid common pitfalls, and notes that explain additional concepts and provide additional information. By working through the 10-minute lessons, you learn everything you need to know quickly and easily!

When you only have time for the answers, Sams Teach Yourself books are your best solution.

Visit **informit.com/samsteachyourself** for a complete listing of the products available.

Try Safari Books Online FREE for 15 days

Get online access to Thousands of Books and Videos

> ## Feed your brain
> Gain unlimited access to thousands of books and videos about technology, digital media and professional development from O'Reilly Media, Addison-Wesley, Microsoft Press, Cisco Press, McGraw Hill, Wiley, WROX, Prentice Hall, Que, Sams, Apress, Adobe Press and other top publishers.

> ## See it, believe it
> Watch hundreds of expert-led instructional videos on today's hottest topics.

WAIT, THERE'S MORE!

> ## Gain a competitive edge
> Be first to learn about the newest technologies and subjects with Rough Cuts pre-published manuscripts and new technology overviews in Short Cuts.

> ## Accelerate your project
> Copy and paste code, create smart searches that let you know when new books about your favorite topics are available, and customize your library with favorites, highlights, tags, notes, mash-ups and more.

* Available to new subscribers only. Discount applies to the Safari Library and is valid for first 12 consecutive monthly billing cycles. Safari Library is not available in all countries.

Brad Miser

Second Edition

Sams Teach Yourself

iCloud

in 10 Minutes

SAMS

Safari
Books Online

FREE
Online Edition

Your purchase of *Sams Teach Yourself iCloud in 10 Minutes* includes access to a free online edition for 45 days through the **Safari Books Online** subscription service. Nearly every Sams book is available online through **Safari Books Online**, along with thousands of books and videos from publishers such as Addison-Wesley Professional, Cisco Press, Exam Cram, IBM Press, O'Reilly Media, Prentice Hall, Que, and VMware Press.

Safari Books Online is a digital library providing searchable, on-demand access to thousands of technology, digital media, and professional development books and videos from leading publishers. With one monthly or yearly subscription price, you get unlimited access to learning tools and information on topics including mobile app and software development, tips and tricks on using your favorite gadgets, networking, project management, graphic design, and much more.

Activate your FREE Online Edition at
informit.com/safarifree

STEP 1: Enter the coupon code: GILWEBI.

STEP 2: New Safari users, complete the brief registration form.
Safari subscribers, just log in.

If you have difficulty registering on Safari or accessing the online edition,
please e-mail customer-service@safaribooksonline.com

Addison Wesley   AdobePress   ALPHA   Cisco Press   FT Press   IBM Press.   Microsoft Press   New Riders   O'REILLY

Peachpit Press   PRENTICE HALL   QUE   Redbooks   SAMS   SAS Publishing   vmware PRESS   WILEY   wrox